Amazing Love

E.G. White

Printed By
Remnant Publications

Amazing Love

This edition published 2000

This book is a compilation of the following books:
The Spirit of Prophecy Vol. 1 & 3 Copyright© 1870
Early Writings Copyright© 1882
Both by E. G. White

ISBN 1-883012-79-1

Preface

In the heart of mankind of whatever race or station in life, there are inexpressible longings for something they do not now possess. This longing is implanted in the very constitution of man by a merciful God, that man may not be satisfied with his present conditions or attainments, whether good or bad. God desires that the human shall seek the best, and find it to the eternal blessing of his soul.

Lucifer, by wily scheme and craft, has perverted these longings of the human heart. He leads men to believe that this desire may be satisfied with pleasure, wealth, ease, fame, or power, but those who have been thus deceived by him find all these things pall upon the sense, leaving the soul as barren and unsatisfied as before. It is God's design that this longing of the human heart shall lead to One who alone is able to satisfy it.

The author of this book, Ellen G. White, (1827-1915) served as the Lord's messenger for seventy years, writing, preaching, counseling, traveling, warning, and encouraging. Her deep spiritual insight and experience will warm your heart and thrill your soul as she reveals the amazing love God has for you. "I have loved thee with an everlasting Love." Jeremiah 31:3.

Contents

1

In the Beginning

Lucifer in Heaven, before his rebellion, was a high and exalted angel, next in honor to God's dear Son. His countenance, like those of the other angels, was mild and expressive of happiness. His forehead was high and broad, showing a powerful intellect. His form was perfect; his bearing noble and majestic. A special light beamed in his countenance, and shone around him brighter and more beautiful than around the other angels; yet Jesus, God's dear Son, had the pre-eminence over all the angelic host. He was one with the Father before the angels were created. Lucifer was envious of Christ, and gradually assumed command which devolved on Christ alone.

The great Creator assembled the heavenly host, that he might in the presence of all the angels confer special honor upon his Son. The Son was seated on the throne with the Father, and the heavenly throng of holy angels was gathered around them. The Father then made known that it was ordained by himself that Christ, his Son, should be equal with himself; so that wherever was the presence of his Son, it was as his own presence. The word of the Son was to be obeyed as readily as the word of the Father. His Son he had invested with authority to command the heavenly host. Especially was his Son to work in union with himself in the anticipated creation of the earth and every living thing that should exist upon the earth. His Son would carry out his will and his purposes, but would do nothing of himself alone. The Father's will would be fulfilled in him.

Lucifer was envious and jealous of Jesus Christ. Yet when all the angels bowed to Jesus to acknowledge his supremacy and high authority and rightful rule, Lucifer bowed with them; but his heart was filled with envy and hatred. Christ had been taken into the special counsel of God in regard to his plans, while Lucifer was unacquainted with them. He did not understand, neither was he permitted to know, the purposes of God. But Christ was acknowledged sovereign of Heaven, his power and authority to be the same as that of God himself. Lucifer thought that he was himself a favorite in Heaven among the angels. He had been highly exalted; but this did not call forth from him gratitude and praise to his Creator. He aspired to the height of God himself. He gloried in his loftiness. He knew that he was honored by the angels. He had a special mission to execute. He had been near the great Creator, and the ceaseless beams of glorious light enshrouding the eternal God, had shone especially upon him. Lucifer thought how angels had obeyed his command with pleasurable alacrity. Were not his garments light and beautiful? Why should Christ thus be honored before himself?

He left the immediate presence of the Father, dissatisfied, and filled with envy against Jesus Christ. Concealing his real purposes, he assembled the angelic host. He introduced his subject, which was himself. As one aggrieved, he related the preference God had given Jesus to the neglect of himself. He told them that henceforth all the sweet liberty the angels had enjoyed was at an end. For had not a ruler been appointed over them, to whom they from henceforth must yield servile honor? He stated to them that he had called them together to assure them that he no longer would submit to this invasion of his rights and theirs; that never would he again bow down to Christ; that he would take the honor upon himself which should have been conferred upon him, and would be the commander of all who would submit to follow him and obey his voice.

There was contention among the angels. Lucifer and his sympathizers were striving to reform the government of God. They were discontented and unhappy because they could not look into his unsearchable wisdom and ascertain his purposes in exalting his Son Jesus, and endowing him with such unlimited power and command. They rebelled against the authority of the Son.

Angels that were loyal and true sought to reconcile this mighty, rebellious angel to the will of his Creator. They justified the act of God in conferring honor upon Jesus Christ, and with forcible reasoning sought to convince Lucifer that no less honor was his now than before the Father had proclaimed the honor which he had conferred upon his Son. They clearly set forth that Jesus was the Son of God, existing with him before the angels were created; and that he had ever stood at the right hand of God, and his mild, loving authority had not heretofore been questioned; and that he had given no commands but what it was joy for the heavenly host to execute. They urged that Christ's receiving special honor from the Father, in the presence of the angels, did not detract from the honor that he had heretofore received. The angels wept. They anxiously sought to move Lucifer to renounce his wicked design and yield submission to their Creator; for all had heretofore been peace and harmony, and what could occasion this dissenting, rebellious voice?

Lucifer refused to listen. And then he turned from the loyal and true angels, denouncing them as slaves. These angels, true to God, stood in amazement as they saw that Lucifer was successful in his effort to excite rebellion. He promised them a new and better government than they then had, in which all would be freedom. Great numbers signified their purpose to accept Lucifer as their leader and chief commander. As he saw his advances were met with success, he flattered himself that he should yet have all the angels on his side, and that he would be equal with God himself, and his voice of authority would be heard in commanding the entire host of Heaven. Again the loyal angels warned Lucifer, and assured him what must be the consequence if he persisted; that He who could create the angels, could by his power overturn all their authority, and in some signal manner punish their audacity and terrible rebellion. To think that an angel should resist the law of God which was as sacred as himself! They warned the rebellious to close their ears to Lucifer's deceptive reasonings, and advised Lucifer, and all who had been affected by him, to go to God and confess their wrong for even admitting a thought of questioning his authority.

Many of Lucifer's sympathizers were inclined to heed the counsel of the loyal angels, and repent of their dissatisfaction, and be again received to the confidence of the Father and his dear Son. The mighty revolter then declared that he was acquainted with God's law, and if he should submit to servile obedience, his honor would be taken from him. No more would he be intrusted with his exalted mission. He told them that himself and they also had now gone too far to go back, and he would brave the consequences; for to bow in servile worship to the Son of God he never would; that God would not forgive, and now they must assert their liberty and gain by force the position and authority which was not willingly accorded to them.*

The loyal angels hasten speedily to the Son of God, and acquaint him with what is taking place among the angels. They find the Father in conference with his beloved Son, to determine the means by which, for the best good of the loyal angels, the assumed authority of Satan could be forever put down. The great God could at once have hurled this arch deceiver from Heaven; but this was not his purpose. He would give the rebellious an equal chance to measure strength and might with his own Son and his loyal angels. In this battle every angel would choose his own side, and be manifested to all. It would

---

*Thus it was that Lucifer, "the light-bearer," the sharer of God's glory, the attendant of his throne, by transgression became Satan, "the adversary."— *Patriarachs and Prophets*, p. 40.

not have been safe to suffer any who united with Satan in his rebellion to continue to occupy Heaven. They had learned the lesson of genuine rebellion against the unchangeable law of God; and this is incurable. If God had exercised his power to punish this chief rebel, disaffected angels would not have been manifested; hence God took another course; for he would manifest distinctly to all the heavenly host his justice and his judgment.

It was the highest crime to rebel against the government of God. All Heaven seemed in commotion. The angels were marshaled in companies, each division with a higher commanding angel at their head. Satan was warring against the law of God, because ambitious to exalt himself, and unwilling to submit to the authority of Gods' Son, Heaven's great commander.

All the heavenly host were summoned to appear before the Father, to have each case determined. Satan unblushingly made known his dissatisfaction that Christ should be preferred before him. He stood up proudly and urged that he should be equal with God, and should be taken into conference with the Father and understand his purposes. God informed Satan that to his Son alone he would reveal his secret purposes, and he required all the family in Heaven, even Satan, to yield him implicit, unquestioned obedience; but that he (Satan) had proved himself unworthy a place in Heaven. Then Satan exultingly pointed to his sympathizers, comprising nearly one half of all the angels, and exclaimed, These are with me! Will you expel these also, and make such a void in Heaven? He then declared that he was prepared to resist the authority of Christ, and to defend his place in Heaven by force of might, strength against strength.

Good angels wept to hear the words of Satan, and his exulting boasts. God declared that the rebellious should remain in Heaven no longer. Their high and happy state had been held upon condition of obedience to the law which God had given to govern the high order of intelligences. But no provision had been made to save those who should venture to transgress his law. Satan grew bold in his rebellion, and expressed his contempt of the Creator's law. This Satan could not bear. He

claimed that angels needed no law; but should be left free to
follow their own will, which would ever guide them right; that
law was a restriction of their liberty, and that to abolish law
was one great object of his standing as he did. The condition
of the angels he thought needed improvement. Not so the mind
of God, who had made laws and exalted them equal to himself. The happiness of the angelic host consisted in their
perfect obedience to law. Each had his special work assigned
him; and until Satan rebelled, there had been perfect order and
harmonious action in Heaven. Then there was war in Heaven.
The Son of God, the Prince of Heaven, and his loyal angels,
engaged in conflict with the arch rebel and those who united
with him. The Son of God and true, loyal angels prevailed; and
Satan and his sympathizers were expelled from heaven. All the
heavenly host acknowledged and adored the God of justice.
Not a taint of rebellion was left in Heaven. All was again peace-
ful and harmonious as before.

Angels in Heaven mourned the fate of those who had been
their companions in happiness and bliss. Their loss was felt in
Heaven. The Father consulted Jesus in regard to at once carry-
ing out their purpose to make man to inhabit the earth. He would
place man upon probation to test his loyalty, before he could
be rendered eternally secure. If he endured the test wherewith
God saw fit to prove him, he should eventually be equal with
the angels. He was to have the favor of God, and he was to
converse with angels, and they with him. He did not see fit to
place them beyond the power of disobedience.

2

The Creation

The Father and the Son engaged in the mighty, wondrous work they had contemplated, of creating the world. The earth came forth from the hand of the Creator exceedingly beautiful. There were mountains, and hills, and plains; and interspersed among them were rivers and bodies of water. The earth was not one extensive plain, but the monotony of the scenery was broken by hills and mountains, not high and ragged as they now are, but regular and beautiful in shape. The bare, high rocks were never seen upon them, but lay beneath the surface, answering as bones to the earth. The waters were regularly dispersed. The hills, mountains, and very beautiful plains, were adorned with plants and flowers, and tall, majestic trees of every description, which were many times larger, and much more beautiful, than trees now are. The air was pure and healthful, and the earth seemed like a noble palace. Angels beheld and rejoiced at the wonderful and beautiful works of God.

After the earth was created, and the beasts upon it, the Father and Son carried out their purpose, which was designed before the fall of Satan, to make man in their own image. They had wrought together in the creation of the earth and every living thing upon it. And now God says to his Son, "Let us make man in our image." As Adam came forth from the hand of his Creator, he was of noble height, and of beautiful symmetry. He was more than twice as tall as men now living upon the earth, and was well proportioned. His features were perfect and beautiful. His complexion was neither white, nor sallow, but ruddy, glowing with the rich tint of health. Eve was not quite as tall as Adam. Her head reached a little above his shoulders. She, too, was noble—perfect in symmetry, and very beautiful.

This sinless pair wore no artificial garments. They were clothed with a covering of light and glory, such as the angels wear. While they lived in obedience to God, this circle of light enshrouded them. Although everything God had made was in the perfection of beauty, and there seemed nothing wanting upon the earth which God had created to make Adam and Eve happy, yet he manifested his great love to them by planting a garden especially for them. A portion of their time was to be occupied in the happy employment of dressing the garden, and a portion in receiving the visits of angels, listening to their instruction, and in happy meditation. Their labor was not wearisome, but pleasant and invigorating. This beautiful garden was to be their home, their special residence.

In this garden the Lord placed trees of every variety for usefulness and beauty. There were trees laden with luxuriant fruit, of rich fragrance, beautiful to the eye, and pleasant to the taste, designed of God to be food for the holy pair. There were the lovely vines which grew upright, laden with their burden of fruit, unlike anything man had seen since the fall. The fruit was very large, and of different colors; some nearly black, some purple, red, pink, and light green. This beautiful and luxuriant growth of fruit upon the branches of the vine was called grapes. They did not trail upon the ground, although not supported by trellises, but the weight of the fruit bowed them down. It was the happy labor of Adam and Eve to form beautiful bowers from the branches of the vine, and train them, forming dwellings of nature's beautiful, living trees and foliage, laden with fragrant fruit.

The earth was clothed with beautiful verdure, while myriads of fragrant flowers of every variety and hue sprang up in rich profusion around them. Everything was tastefully and gloriously arranged. In the midst of the garden stood the tree of life, the glory of which surpassed all other trees. Its fruit looked like apples of gold and silver, and was to perpetuate immortality. The leaves contained healing properties.

Very happy were the holy pair in Eden. Unlimited control was given them over every living thing. The lion and the lamb sported together peacefully and harmlessly around them, or slumbered at their feet. Birds of every variety of color and plumage flitted among the trees and flowers, and about Adam and Eve, while their mellow-toned music echoed among the trees in sweet accord to the praises of their Creator.

Adam and Eve were charmed with the beauties of their Eden home. They were delighted with the little songsters around them, wearing their bright yet graceful plumage, and warbling forth their happy, cheerful music. The holy pair united with them and raised their voices in harmonious songs of love, praise and adoration, to the Father and his dear Son, for the tokens of love which surrounded them. They recognized the order and harmony of creation, which spoke of wisdom and knowledge that were infinite. Some new beauty and additional glory of their Eden home they were continually discovering, which filled their hearts with deeper love, and brought from their lips expressions of gratitude and reverence to their Creator.

3

The Temptation and Fall

In the midst of the garden, near the tree of life, stood the tree of knowledge of good and evil. This tree was especially designed of God to be the pledge of their obedience, faith and love to him. Of this tree the Lord commanded our first parents not to eat, neither to touch it, lest they die. He told them that they might freely eat of all the trees in the garden except one; but if they ate of that tree they should surely die.

When Adam and Eve were placed in the beautiful garden, they had everything for their happiness which they could desire. But he chose, in his all-wise arrangements, to test their loyalty before they could be rendered eternally secure. They were to have his favor, and he was to converse with them, and they with him. Yet he did not place evil out of their reach. Satan was permitted to tempt them. If they endured the trial, they were to be in perpetual favor with God and the heavenly angels.

Satan stood in amazement at his new condition. His happiness was gone. He looked upon the angels who, with him, were once so happy, but who had been expelled from Heaven with him. Before their fall, not a shade of discontent had marred their perfect bliss. Now all seemed changed. Countenances which had reflected the image of their Maker were gloomy and despairing. Strife, discord, and bitter recrimination, were among them. Previous to their rebellion these things had been unknown in Heaven. Satan now beholds the terrible results of his rebellion. He shuddered, and feared to face the future, and to contemplate the end of these things.

The hour for joyful, happy songs of praise to God and his dear Son had come. Satan had led the heavenly choir. He had raised the first note, then all the angelic host united with him, and glorious strains of music had resounded through Heaven in honor of God and his dear Son. But now, instead of strains of sweetest music, discord and angry words fall upon the ear of the great rebel leader. Where was he? Was it not all a horrible dream? Was he shut out of Heaven? Were the gates of Heaven never more to open and admit him? The hour of worship draws nigh, when bright and holy angels bow before the Father. No more will he unite in heavenly song. No more will he bow in reverence and holy awe before the presence of the eternal God. Could he be again as he was when he was pure, true and loyal, gladly would he yield up the claims of his authority. But he was lost! beyond redemption, for his presumptuous rebellion! And this was not all; he had led others to rebellion and to the same lost condition with himself—angels, who had never thought to question the will of Heaven, or refuse obedience to the law of God till he had put it into their minds, presenting before them that they might enjoy a greater good, a higher and more glorious liberty. This had been the sophistry whereby he had deceived them. A responsibility now rests upon him from which he would fain be released.

These spirits had become turbulent with disappointed hopes. Instead of greater good, they were experiencing the sad results of disobedience and disregard of law. Never more would these unhappy beings be swayed by the mild rule of Jesus Christ. Never more would their spirits be stirred by the deep, earnest love, peace, and joy, which his presence had ever inspired in them, to be returned to him in cheerful obedience and reverential honor.

Satan trembled as he viewed his work. He was alone in meditation upon the past, the present, and his future plans. His mighty frame shook as with a tempest. An angel from Heaven was passing. He called him, and entreated an interview with

Christ. This was granted him. He then related to the Son of God that he repented of his rebellion, and wished again the favor of God. He was willing to take the place God had previously assigned him, and be under his wise command. Christ wept at Satan's woe, but told him, as the mind of God, that he could never be received into Heaven. Heaven must not be placed in jeopardy. All Heaven would be marred should he be received back; for sin and rebellion originated with him. The seeds of rebellion were still within him. He had, in his rebellion, no occasion for his course, and he had not only hopelessly ruined himself, but the host of angels also, who would then have been happy in Heaven had he remained steadfast. The law of God could condemn, but could not pardon.

He repented not of his rebellion because he saw the goodness of God which he had abused. It was not possible that his love for God had so increased since his fall that it would lead to cheerful submission and happy obedience to his law which had been despised. The wretchedness he realized in losing the sweet light of Heaven, and the sense of guilt which forced itself upon him, and the disappointment he experienced himself in not finding his expectations realized, were the cause of his grief. To be commander out of Heaven, was vastly different from being thus honored in Heaven. The loss he had sustained of all the privileges of Heaven seemed too much to be borne. He wished to regain these.

This great change of position had not increased his love for God, nor for his wise and just law. When Satan become fully convinced that there was no possibility of his being reinstated in the favor of God, he manifested his malice with increased hatred and fiery vehemence.

God knew that such determined rebellion would not remain inactive. Satan would invent means to annoy the heavenly angels, and show contempt for his authority. As he could not gain admission within the gates of Heaven, he would wait just at the entrance, to taunt the angels and seek contention with them as they went in and out. He would seek to destroy the happiness of Adam and Eve. He would endeavor to incite them to rebellion, knowing that this would cause grief in heaven.

His followers were seeking him; and he aroused himself and, assuming a look of defiance, informed them of his plans to wrest from God the noble Adam and his companion Eve. If he could, in any way, beguile them to disobedience, God would make some provision whereby they might be pardoned, and then himself and all the fallen angels would be in a fair way to share with them of God's mercy. If this should fail, they could unite with Adam and Eve; for when once they should transgress the law of God, they would be subjects of God's wrath, like themselves. Their transgression would place them also, in a state of rebellion; and they could unite with Adam and Eve, take possession of Eden, and hold it as their home. And if they could gain access to the tree of life in the midst of the garden, their strength would, they thought, be equal to that of the holy angels, and even God himself could not expel them.

Satan held a consultation with his evil angels. They did not all readily unite to engage in this hazardous and terrible work. He told them that he would not intrust any one of them to accomplish this work; for he thought that he alone had wisdom sufficient to carry forward so important an enterprise. He wished them to consider the matter while he should leave them and seek retirement, to mature his plans. He sought to impress upon them that this was their last and only hope. If they failed here, all prospect of regaining and controlling Heaven, or any part of God's creation, was hopeless.

Satan went alone to mature plans that would most surely secure the fall of Adam and Eve. He had fears that his purposes might be defeated. And again, even if he should be successful in leading Adam and Eve to disobey the commandment of God, and thus become transgressors of his law, and no good come to himself, his own case would not be improved; his guilt would only be increased.

He shuddered at the thought of plunging the holy, happy pair into the misery and remorse he was himself enduring. He

seemed in a state of indecision; at one time firm and determined, then hesitating and wavering. His angels were seeking
him, their leader, to acquaint him with their decision. They will
unite with Satan in his plans, and with him bear the responsibility, and share the consequences.

Satan cast off his feelings of despair and weakness, and,
as their leader, fortified himself to brave out the matter, and
do all in his power to defy the authority of God and his Son.
He acquainted them with his plans. If he should come boldly
upon Adam and Eve and make complaints of God's own Son,
they would not listen to him for a moment, but would be prepared for such an attack. Should he seek to intimidate them
because of his power, so recently an angel in high authority,
he could accomplish nothing. He decided that cunning and deceit would do what might, or force, could not.

God assembled the angelic host to take measures to avert
the threatened evil. It was decided in Heaven's council for angels to visit Eden and warn Adam that he was in danger from
the foe. Two angels sped on their way to visit our first parents.
The holy pair received them with joyful innocence, expressing
their grateful thanks to their Creator for thus surrounding them
with such a profusion of his bounty. Everything lovely and attractive was theirs to enjoy, and everything seemed wisely
adapted to their wants; and that which they prized above all
other blessings, was the society of the Son of God and the heavenly angels, for they had much to relate to them at every visit,
of their new discoveries of the beauties of nature in their lovely
Eden home, and they had many questions to ask relative to many
things which they could but indistinctly comprehend.

The angels graciously and lovingly gave them the information they desired. They also gave them the sad history of
Satan's rebellion and fall. They then distinctly informed them
that the tree of knowledge was placed in the garden to be a
pledge of their obedience and love to God; that the high and
happy estate of the holy angels was to be retained upon condition
of obedience; that they were similarly situated; that they could

obey the law of God and be inexpressibly happy, or disobey, and lose their high estate, and be plunged into hopeless despair.

They told Adam and Eve that God would not compel them to obey—that he had not removed from them power to go contrary to his will; that they were moral agents, free to obey or disobey. There was but one prohibition that God had seen fit to lay upon them as yet. If they should transgress the will of God, they would surely die. They told Adam and Eve that the most exalted angel, next in order to Christ, refused obedience to the law of God which he had ordained to govern heavenly beings; that this rebellion had caused war in Heaven which resulted in the rebellious being expelled therefrom, and every angel was driven out of Heaven who united with him in questioning the authority of the great Jehovah; and that this fallen foe was now an enemy to all that concerned the interest of God and his dear Son.

They told them that Satan purposed to do them harm, and it was necessary for them to be guarded, for they might come in contact with the fallen foe; but he could not harm them while they yielded obedience to God's command; for, if necessary, every angel from Heaven would come to their help rather than that he should in any way do them harm. But if they disobeyed the command of God, then Satan would have power to ever annoy, perplex, and trouble, them. If they remained steadfast against the first insinuations of Satan, they were as secure as the heavenly angels. But if they yielded to the tempter, He who spared not the exalted angels, would not spare them. They must suffer the penalty of their transgression; for the law of God was as sacred as himself, and he required implicit obedience from all in Heaven and on earth.

The angels cautioned Eve not to separate from her husband in her employment; for she might be brought in contact with this fallen foe. If separated from each other, they would be in greater danger than if both were together. The angels charged them to closely follow the instructions God had given them in reference to the tree of knowledge; for in perfect obedience they were safe, and this fallen foe could then have no power to deceive them. God would not permit Satan to follow the holy pair with continual temptations. He could have access to them only at the tree of knowledge of good and evil.

Adam and Eve assured the angels that they should never transgress the express command of God; for it was their highest pleasure to do his will. The angels united with Adam and Eve in holy strains of harmonious music; and as their songs pealed forth from blissful Eden, Satan heard the sound of their strains of joyful adoration to the Father and Son. And as Satan heard it, his envy, hatred, and malignity, increased, and he expressed his anxiety to his followers to incite them (Adam and Eve) to disobedience, and at once bring down the wrath of God upon them, and change their songs of praise to hatred, and curses to their Maker.

Satan assumes the form of a serpent, and enters Eden. The serpent was a beautiful creature, with wings; and while flying through the air, his appearance was bright, resembling burnished gold. He did not go upon the ground, but went from place to place through the air, and ate fruit like man. Satan entered into the serpent, and took his position in the tree of knowledge, and commenced leisurely eating of the fruit.

Eve, unconsciously at first, separated from her husband in her employment. When she became aware of the fact, she felt that there might be danger; but again she thought herself secure, even if she did not remain close by the side of her husband. She had wisdom and strength to know if evil came, and to meet it. This the angels had cautioned her not to do. Eve found herself gazing with mingled curiosity and admiration upon the fruit of the forbidden tree. She saw it was very lovely, and was reasoning with herself why God had so decidedly prohibited their eating or touching it. Now was Satan's opportunity. He addressed her as though he was able to divine her thoughts: "Yea, hath God said, Ye shall not eat of every tree of the garden?" Thus, with soft and pleasant words, and with musical voice, he addressed the wondering Eve. She was startled to hear a serpent speak. He extolled her beauty and exceeding loveliness, which was not displeasing to Eve. But she was amazed, for she knew that to the serpent God had not given the power of speech.

Eve's curiosity was aroused. Instead of fleeing from the spot, she listened to hear a serpent talk. It did not occur to her mind that it might be that fallen foe, using the serpent as a medium. It was Satan that spoke, not the serpent. Eve was beguiled, flattered, infatuated. Had she met a commanding personage, possessing a form like the angels, and resembling them, she would have been upon her guard. But that strange voice should have driven her to her husband's side to inquire of him why another should thus freely address her. But she enters into a controversy with the serpent. She answers his question, "We may eat of the fruit of the trees of the garden. But of the fruit of the tree which is in the midst of the garden, God hath said, Ye shall not eat of it, neither shall ye touch it, lest ye die." The serpent answers, "Ye shall not surely die; for God doth know that in the day ye eat thereof, then your eyes shall be opened, and ye shall be as gods, knowing good and evil."

Satan would convey the idea that by eating of the forbidden tree, they would receive a new and more noble kind of knowledge than they had hitherto attained. This has been his special work with great success ever since his fall, to lead men to pry into the secrets of the Almighty, and not to be satisfied with what God has revealed, and not careful to obey that which he has commanded. He would lead them to disobey God's commands, and then make them believe that they are entering a wonderful field of knowledge. This is purely supposition, and a miserable deception. They fail to understand what God has revealed, and disregard his explicit commandments, and aspire after wisdom, independent of God, and seek to understand that which he has been pleased to withhold from mortals. They are elated with their ideas of progression, and charmed with their own vain philosophy; but grope in midnight darkness relative to true knowledge. They are ever learning, and never able to come to the knowledge of the truth.

It was not the will of God that this sinless pair should have
any knowledge of evil. He had freely given them the good, but
withheld the evil. Eve thought the words of the serpent wise,
and she received the broad assertion, "Ye shall not surely die;
for God doth know that in the day ye eat thereof then your
eyes shall be opened, and ye shall be as gods knowing good
and evil"—making God a liar. Satan boldly insinuates that God
had deceived them to keep them from being exalted in knowledge equal with himself. God said, If ye eat "ye shall surely
die." The serpent said, If ye eat "ye shall not surely die."

The tempter assured Eve that as soon as she ate of the fruit
she would receive a new and superior knowledge that would
make her equal with God. He called her attention to himself.
He ate freely of the tree and found it not only perfectly harm-
less, but delicious and exhilarating; and told her that it was
because of its wonderful properties to impart wisdom and power
that God had prohibited them from tasting or even touching it;
for he knew its wonderful qualities. He stated that by eating of
the fruit of the tree forbidden them was the reason he had attained the power of speech. He intimated that God would not
carry out his word. It was merely a threat to intimidate them
and keep them from great good. He further told them that they
could not die. Had they not eaten of the tree of life which per-
petuates immortality? He said that God was deceiving them to
keep them from a higher state of felicity and more exalted happiness. The tempter plucked the fruit and passed it to Eve. She
took it in her hand. Now, said the tempter, you were prohibited
from even touching it lest you die. He told her that she would
realize no more sense of evil and death in eating than in touching or handling the fruit. Eve was emboldened because she felt
not the immediate signs of God's displeasure. She thought the
words of the tempter all wise and correct. She ate, and was
delighted with the fruit. It seemed delicious to her taste, and
she imagined that she realized in herself the wonderful effects
of the fruit.

She then plucked for herself of the fruit and ate, and imagined she felt the quickening power of a new and elevated existence as the result of the exhilarating influence of the forbidden fruit. She was in a strange and unnatural excitement as she sought her husband, with her hands filled with the forbidden fruit. She related to him the wise discourse of the serpent, and wished to conduct him at once to the tree of knowledge. She told him she had eaten of the fruit, and instead of her feeling any sense of death, she realized a pleasing, exhilarating influence. As soon as Eve had disobeyed, she became a powerful medium through which to occasion the fall of her husband.

I saw a sadness come over the countenance of Adam. He appeared afraid and astonished. A struggle appeared to be going on in his mind. He told Eve he was quite certain that this was the foe that they had been warned against; and if so, that she must die. She assured him she felt no ill effects, but rather a very pleasant influence, and entreated him to eat.

Adam quite well understood that his companion had transgressed the only prohibition laid upon them as a test of their fidelity and love. Eve reasoned that the serpent said they should not surely die, and his words must be true, for she felt no signs of God's displeasure, but a pleasant influence, as she imagined the angels felt. Adam regretted that Eve had left his side; but now the deed was done. He must be separated from her whose society he had loved so well. How could he have it thus? His love for Eve was strong. And in utter discouragement he resolved to share her fate. He reasoned that Eve was a part of himself; and if she must die, he would die with her; for he could not bear the thought of separation from her. He lacked faith in his merciful and benevolent Creator. He did not think that God, who had formed him out of the dust of the ground into a living, beautiful form, and had created Eve to be his companion, could supply her place. After all, might not the words of this wise serpent be correct? Eve was before him, just as lovely and beautiful, and apparently as innocent, as before this act of disobedience. She expressed greater, higher love for him than before her disobedience, as the effects of the fruit she had eaten. He saw in her no signs of death. She had told him of the happy influence of the fruit, of her ardent love for him, and he decided to brave the consequences. He seized the fruit and quickly ate it, and, like Eve, felt not immediately its ill effects.

Eve had thought herself capable of deciding between right and wrong. The flattering hope of entering a higher state of knowledge had led her to think that the serpent was her especial friend, possessing a great interest in her welfare. Had she sought her husband, and they had related to their Maker the words of the serpent, they would have been delivered at once from his artful temptation.

God instructed our first parents in regard to the tree of knowledge, and they were fully informed relative to the fall of Satan, and the danger of listening to his suggestions. He did not deprive them of the power of eating the forbidden fruit. He left them as free moral agents to believe his word, obey his commandments and live, or believe the tempter, disobey and perish. They both ate, and the great wisdom they obtained was the knowledge of sin, and a sense of guilt. The covering of light about them soon disappeared, and under a sense of guilt, and loss of their divine covering, a shivering seized them, and they tried to cover their exposed forms. The Lord would not have them investigate the fruit of the tree of knowledge, for then they would be exposed to Satan masked. He knew that they would be perfectly safe if they touched not the fruit.

Our first parents chose to believe the words, as they thought, of a serpent; yet he had given them no tokens of his love. He had done nothing for their happiness and benefit; while God had given them everything that was good for food, and pleasant to the sight. Everywhere the eye might rest was abundance and beauty; yet Eve was deceived by the serpent, to think that there was something withheld which would make them wise, even as God. Instead of believing and confiding in God, she basely distrusted his goodness, and cherished the words of Satan.

After Adam's transgression he at first imagined that he felt the rising to a new and higher existence. But soon the thought of his transgression terrified him. The air that had been of a mild and even temperature, seemed to chill them. The guilty pair had a sense of sin. They felt a dread of the future, a sense of want, a nakedness of soul. The sweet love, and peace, and happy, contented bliss, seemed removed from them, and in its place a want of something came over them that they never experienced before. They then for the first turned their attention to the external. They had not been clothed, but were draped in light as were the heavenly angels. This light which had enshrouded them departed. To relieve the sense of lack and nakedness which they realized, their attention was directed to seek a covering for their forms; for how could they meet the eye of God and angels unclothed?

Their crime is now before them in its true light. Their transgression of God's express command assumes a clearer character. Adam censured Eve's folly in leaving his side, and being deceived by the serpent. They both flattered themselves that God, who had given them everything to make them happy, might yet excuse their disobedience, because of his great love to them, and that their punishment would not be so dreadful, after all.

Satan exulted in his success. He had now tempted the woman to distrust God, to question his wisdom, and to seek to penetrate his all-wise plans. And through her he had also caused the overthrow of Adam, who, in consequence of his love for Eve, disobeyed the command of God, and fell with her.

The news of man's fall spread through Heaven—every harp was hushed. The angels cast their crowns from their heads in sorrow. All Heaven was in agitation. The angels were grieved at the base ingratitude of man, in return for the rich bounties God had provided. A council was held to decide what must be done with the guilty pair. The angels feared that they would put forth the hand, and eat of the tree of life, and thus perpetuate a life of sin.

The Lord visited Adam and Eve, and made known to them the consequence of their disobedience. As they hear God's majestic approach, they seek to hide themselves from his inspection, whom they delighted, while in their innocence and holiness, to meet. "And the Lord God called unto Adam, and said unto him, Where art thou? And he said, I heard thy voice in the garden, and I was afraid because I was naked, and I hid myself. And he said, Who told thee that thou wast naked? Hast thou eaten of the tree whereof I commanded thee that thou shouldest not eat?" This question was asked by the Lord, not because he needed information, but for the conviction of the guilty pair. How didst thou become ashamed and fearful? Adam acknowledged his transgression, not because he was penitent for his great disobedience, but to cast reflection upon God. "The woman whom thou gavest to be with me, she gave me of the tree, and I did eat." The woman was then addressed: "What is this that thou hast done?" Eve answered, "The serpent beguiled me, and I did eat." The Lord then addressed the serpent: "Because thou has done this, thou art cursed above all cattle, and above every beast of the field: upon thy belly shalt thou go, and dust shalt thou eat all the days of thy life." As the serpent had been exalted above the beasts of the field, he should be degraded beneath them all, and be detested by man, inasmuch as he was the medium through which Satan acted. "And unto Adam he said, Because thou hast hearkened unto the voice of thy wife, and hast eaten of the tree of which I commanded thee, saying, Thou shalt not eat of it, cursed is the ground for thy sake; in sorrow shalt thou eat of it all the days of thy life; thorns also and thistles shall it bring forth to thee; and thou shalt eat the herb of the field. In the sweat of thy face shalt thou eat bread till thou return unto the ground."

God cursed the ground because of their sin in eating of the tree of knowledge, and declared, "In sorrow shalt thou eat of it all the days of thy life." He had apportioned them the good, but withheld the evil. Now God declares that they shall eat of it, that is, they should be acquainted with evil all the days of their life.

The race from that time forward was to be afflicted by Satan's temptations. A life of perpetual toil and anxiety was appointed unto Adam, instead of the happy, cheerful labor he had hitherto enjoyed. They should be subject to disappointment, grief and pain, and finally come to dissolution. They were made of the dust of the earth, and unto dust should they return.

They were informed that they would have to lose their Eden home. They had yielded to Satan's deception and believed the word of Satan, that God would lie. By their transgression they had opened a way for Satan to gain access to them more readily, and it was not safe for them to remain in the garden of Eden, lest in their state of sin, they gain access to the tree of life, and perpetuate a life of sin. They entreated to be permitted to remain, although they acknowledged that they had forfeited all right to blissful Eden. They promised that they would in the future yield to God implicit obedience. They were informed that in their fall from innocence to guilt, they gained no strength but great weakness. They had not preserved their integrity while they were in a state of holy, happy innocence, and they would have far less strength to remain true and loyal in a state of conscious guilt. They were filled with keenest anguish and remorse. They now realized that the penalty of sin was death.

Angels were commissioned to immediately guard the way of the tree of life. It was Satan's studied plan that Adam and Eve should disobey God, receive his frown, and then partake of the tree of life, that they might perpetuate a life of sin. But holy angels were sent to debar their way to the tree of life. Around these angels flashed beams of light on every side, which had the appearance of glittering swords.

4

The Plan of Salvation

Sorrow filled Heaven, as it was realized that man was lost, and the world that God created was to be filled with mortals doomed to misery, sickness, and death, and there was no way of escape for the offender. The whole family of Adam must die. I saw the lovely Jesus, and beheld an expression of sympathy and sorrow upon his countenance. Soon I saw him approach the exceeding bright light which enshrouded the Father. Said my accompanying angel, He is in close converse with his Father. The anxiety of the angels seemed to be intense while Jesus was communing with his Father. Three times he was shut in by the glorious light about the Father, and the third time he came from the Father his person could be seen. His countenance was calm, free from all perplexity and trouble, and shone with benevolence and loveliness, such as words cannot express.He then made known to the angelic host that a way of escape had been made for lost man. He told them that he had been pleading with his Father, and had offered to give his life a ransom, and take the sentence of death upon himself, that through him man might find pardon; that through the merits of his blood, and obedience to the law of God, they could have the favor of God, and be brought into the beautiful garden, and eat of the fruit of the tree of life.

At first the angels could not rejoice, for their commander concealed nothing from them, but opened before them the plan of salvation. Jesus told them that he would stand between the wrath of his Father and guilty man, that he would bear iniquity and scorn, and but few would receive him as the Son of God. Nearly all would hate and reject him. He would leave all his glory in Heaven, appear upon earth as a man, humble himself as a man, become acquainted by his own experience with the various temptations with which man would be beset, that he might know how to succor those who should be tempted; and that finally, after his mission as a teacher should be accomplished, he would be delivered into the hands of men, and endure almost every cruelty and suffering that Satan and his angels could inspire wicked men to inflict; that he should die the cruelest of deaths, hung up between the heavens and the earth as a guilty sinner; that he should suffer dreadful hours of agony, which even angels could not look upon, but would vail their faces from the sight. Not merely agony of body would he suffer; but mental agony, that with which bodily suffering could in no wise be compared. The weight of the sins of the whole world would be upon him. He told them he would die, and rise again the third day, and should ascend to his Father to intercede for wayward, guilty man.

The angels prostrated themselves before him. They offered their lives. Jesus said to them that he should by his death save many; that the life of an angel could not pay the debt. His life alone could be accepted of his Father as a ransom for man. Jesus also told them that they should have a part to act, to be with him, and at different times strengthen him. That he should take man's fallen nature, and his strength would not be even equal with theirs. And they should be witnesses of his humiliation and great sufferings. And as they should witness his sufferings, and the hate of men towards him, they would be stirred with the deepest emotions, and through their love for him, would wish to rescue and deliver him from his murderers; but that they must not interfere to prevent anything they should behold; and that they should act a part in his resurrection; that the plan of salvation was devised, and his Father had accepted the plan.

With a holy sadness Jesus comforted and cheered the angels, and informed them that hereafter those whom he should redeem would be with him, and ever dwell with him; and that by his death he should ransom many, and destroy him who had the power of death. And his Father would give him the kingdom, and the greatness of the kingdom under the whole heaven, and he should possess it forever and ever. Satan and sinners should be destroyed, never more to disturb Heaven, or the purified new earth. Jesus bade the heavenly host be reconciled to the plan that his Father accepted, and rejoice that fallen man could be exalted again through his death, to obtain favor with God and enjoy Heaven.

Then joy, inexpressible joy, filled Heaven. And the heavenly host sung a song of praise and adoration. They touched their harps and sung a note higher than they had done before, for the great mercy and condescension of God in yielding up his dearly Beloved to die for a race of rebels. Praise and adoration were poured forth for the self-denial and sacrifice of Jesus; that he would consent to leave the bosom of his Father, and choose a life of suffering and anguish, and die an ignominious death to give his life for others.

Said the angel, Think ye that the Father yielded up his dearly beloved Son without a struggle? No, no. It was even a struggle with the God of Heaven, whether to let guilty man perish, or to give his beloved Son to die for them. Angels were so interested for man's salvation that there could be found among them those who would yield their glory, and give their life for perishing man. But, said my accompanying angel, That would avail nothing. The transgression was so great that an angel's life would not pay the debt. Nothing but the death and intercessions of his Son would pay the debt, and save lost man from hopeless sorrow and misery.

But the work of the angels was assigned them, to ascend and descend with strengthening balm from glory to soothe the Son of God in his sufferings, and administer unto him. Also, their work would be to guard and keep the subjects of grace from the evil angels, and the darkness constantly thrown around them by Satan. I saw that it was impossible for God to alter or change his law, to save lost, perishing man; therefore he suffered his beloved Son to die for man's transgression.

Satan again rejoiced with his angels that he could, by causing man's fall, pull down the Son of God from his exalted position. He told his angels that when Jesus should take fallen man's nature, he could overpower him, and hinder the accomplishment of the plan of salvation.

I was then shown Satan as he was, a happy, exalted angel. Then I was shown him as he now is. He still bears a kingly form. His features are still noble, for he is an angel fallen. But the expression of his countenance is full of anxiety, care, unhappiness, malice, hate, mischief, deceit, and every evil. That brow which was once so noble, I particularly noticed. His forehead commenced from his eyes to recede backward. I saw that he had demeaned himself so long that every good quality was debased, and every evil trait was developed. His eyes were cunning and sly, and showed great penetration. His frame was large; but the flesh hung loosely about his hands and face. As I beheld him, his chin was resting upon his left hand. He appeared to be in deep thought. A smile was upon his countenance, which made me tremble, it was so full of evil and Satanic slyness. This smile is the one he wears just before he makes sure of his victim; and as he fastens the victim in his snare, this smile grows horrible.

In humility and inexpressible sadness, Adam and Eve left the lovely garden wherein they had been so happy until they disobeyed the command of God. The atmosphere was changed. It was no longer unvarying as before the transgression. God clothed them with coats of skins to protect them from the sense of chilliness and then of heat to which they were exposed.

All Heaven mourned on account of the disobedience and fall of Adam and Eve, which brought the wrath of God upon the whole human race. They were cut off from communing with God, and were plunged in hopeless misery. The law of God could not be changed to meet man's necessity; for in God's arrangement it was never to lose its force, nor give up the smallest part of its claims.

The angels of God were commissioned to visit the fallen pair and inform them that although they could no longer retain possession of their holy estate, their Eden home, because of their transgression of the law of God, yet their case was not altogether hopeless. They were then informed that the Son of God, who had conversed with them in Eden, had been moved with pity as he viewed their hopeless condition, and had volunteered to take upon himself the punishment due to them, and die for them that man might yet live, through faith in the atonement Christ proposed to make for him. Through Christ a door of hope was opened, that man, notwithstanding his great sin, should not be under the absolute control of Satan. Faith in the merits of the Son of God would so elevate man that he could resist the devices of Satan. Probation would be granted him in which, through a life of repentance, and faith in the atonement of the Son of God, he might be redeemed from his transgression of the Father's law, and thus be elevated to a position where his efforts to keep his law could be accepted.

The angels related to them the grief that was felt in Heaven, as it was announced that they had transgressed the law of God, which had made it expedient for Christ to make the great sacrifice of his own precious life.

When Adam and Eve realized how exalted and sacred was the law of God, the transgression of which made so costly a sacrifice necessary to save them and their posterity from utter ruin, they plead to die themselves, or to let them and their posterity endure the penalty of their transgression, rather than that the beloved Son of God should make this great sacrifice. The anguish of Adam was increased. He saw that his sins were of so great magnitude as to involve fearful consequences. And must it be that Heaven's honored Commander, who had walked with him, and talked with him, while in his holy innocence, whom angels honored and worshiped, must be brought down from his exalted position to die because of his transgression.

Adam was informed that an angel's life could not pay the debt. The law of Jehovah, the foundation of his government in Heaven and upon earth, was as sacred as God himself; and for this reason the life of an angel could not be accepted of God as a sacrifice for its transgression. His law was of more importance in his sight than the holy angels around his throne. The Father could not abolish nor change one precept of his law to meet man in his fallen condition. But the Son of God, who had in unison with the Father created man, could make an atonement for man acceptable to God, by giving his life a sacrifice, and bearing the wrath of his Father. Angels informed Adam that, as his transgression had brought death and wretchedness, life and immortality would be brought to light through the sacrifice of Jesus Christ.

To Adam were revealed future, important events, from his expulsion from Eden to the flood, and onward to the first advent of Christ upon the earth. His love for Adam and his posterity would lead the Son of God to condescend to take human nature, and thus elevate, through his own humiliation, all who would believe on him. Such a sacrifice was of sufficient value to save the whole world; but only a few would avail themselves of the salvation brought to them through such a wonderful sacrifice. The many would not comply with the conditions required of them that they might be partakers of his great salvation. They would prefer sin and transgression of the law of God, rather than repentance and obedience, relying by faith upon the merits of the sacrifice offered. This sacrifice was of such infinite value as to make a man who should avail himself of it, more precious than fine gold, even a man than the golden wedge of Ophir.

Adam was carried down through successive generations, and saw the increase of crime, of guilt and defilement, because man would yield to his naturally strong inclinations to transgress the holy law of God. He was shown the curse of God resting more and more heavily upon the human race, upon the

cattle, and upon the earth, because of man's continued transgression. He was shown that iniquity and violence would
steadily increase; yet amid all the tide of human misery and
woe, there would ever be a few who would preserve the knowledge of God, and would remain unsullied amid the prevailing
moral degeneracy. Adam was made to comprehend what sin
is—the transgression of the law. He was shown that moral,
mental, and physical degeneracy would result to the race, from
transgression, until the world would be filled with human misery of every type.

The days of man were shortened by his own course of sin
in transgressing the righteous law of God. The race was finally
so greatly depreciated that they appeared inferior, and almost
valueless. They were generally incompetent to appreciate the
mystery of Calvary, the grand and elevated facts of the atonement and the plan of salvation, because of the indulgence of
the carnal mind. Yet, notwithstanding the weakness, and en-
feebled mental, moral and physical, powers of the human race,
Christ, true to the purpose for which he left Heaven, continues
his interest in the feeble, depreciated, degenerate specimens
of humanity, and invites them to hide their weakness and great
deficiencies in him. If they will come unto him, he will supply
all their needs.

When Adam, according to God's special directions, made
an offering for sin, it was to him a most painful ceremony. His
hand must be raised to take life, which God alone could give,
and make an offering for sin. It was the first time he had witnessed death. As he looked upon the bleeding victim, writhing
in the agonies of death, he was to look forward by faith to the
Son of God, whom the victim prefigured, who was to die man's
sacrifice.

This ceremonial offering, ordained of God, was to be a perpetual reminder to Adam of his guilt, and also a penitential
acknowledgment of his sin. This act of taking life gave Adam
a deeper and more perfect sense of his transgression, which
nothing less than the death of God's dear Son could expiate.

He marveled at the infinite goodness and matchless love which would give such a ransom to save the guilty. As Adam was slaying the innocent victim, it seemed to him that he was shedding the blood of the Son of God by his own hand. He knew that if he had remained steadfast to God, and true to his holy law, there would have been no death of beast nor of man. Yet in the sacrificial offerings, pointing to the great and perfect offering of God's dear Son, there appeared a star of hope to illuminate the dark and terrible future, and relieve it of its utter hopelessness and ruin.

In the beginning, the head of each family was considered ruler and priest of his own household. Afterward, as the race multiplied upon the earth, men of divine appointment performed this solemn worship of sacrifice for the people. The blood of beasts was to be associated in the minds of sinners with the blood of the Son of God. The death of the victim was to evidence to all that the penalty of sin was death. By the act of sacrifice, the sinner acknowledged his guilt, and manifested his faith, looking forward to the great and perfect sacrifice of the Son of God, which the offering of beasts prefigured. Without the atonement of the Son of God there could be no communication of blessing, or salvation from God to man. God was jealous for the honor of his law. The transgression of that law caused a fearful separation between God and man. To Adam in his innocency was granted communion, direct, free and happy, with his Maker. After his transgression, God would communicate to man through Christ and angels.

5

The First Advent of Christ

I was carried down to the time when Jesus was to take upon Himself man's nature, humble Himself as a man, and suffer the temptations of Satan.

His birth was without worldly grandeur. He was born in a stable and cradled in a manger; yet His birth was honored far above that of any of the sons of men. Angels from heaven informed the shepherds of the advent of Jesus, and light and glory from God accompanied their testimony. The heavenly host touched their harps and glorified God. They triumphantly heralded the advent of the Son of God to a fallen world to accomplish the work of redemption, and by His death to bring peace, happiness, and everlasting life to man. God honored the advent of His Son. Angels worshiped Him.

Angels of God hovered over the scene of His baptism; the Holy Spirit descended in the form of a dove and lighted upon Him, and as the people stood greatly amazed, with their eyes fastened upon Him, the Father's voice was heard from heaven, saying, Thou art My beloved Son; in Thee I am well pleased.

John was not certain that it was the Saviour who came to be baptized of him in Jordan. But God had promised him a sign by which he should know the Lamb of God. That sign was given as the heavenly dove rested upon Jesus, and the glory of God shone round about Him. John reached forth his hand, pointing to Jesus, and with a loud voice cried out, "Behold the Lamb of God, which taketh away the sin of the world!"

John informed his disciples that Jesus was the promised Messiah, the Saviour of the world. As his work was closing, he taught his disciples to look to Jesus, and follow Him as the Great Teacher. John's life was sorrowful and self-denying. He heralded the first advent of Christ, but was not permitted to witness His miracles, and enjoy the power manifested by Him. When Jesus should establish Himself as a teacher, John knew that he himself must die. His voice was seldom heard, except in the wilderness. His life was lonely. He did not cling to his father's family, to enjoy their society, but left them in order to fulfill his mission. Multitudes left the busy cities and villages and flocked to the wilderness to hear the words of the wonderful prophet. John laid the ax to the root of the tree. He reproved sin, fearless of consequences, and prepared the way for the Lamb of God.

Herod was affected as he listened to the powerful, pointed testimonies of John, and with deep interest he inquired what he must do to become his disciple. John was acquainted with the fact that he was about to marry his brother's wife, while her husband was yet living, and faithfully told Herod that this was not lawful. Herod was unwilling to make any sacrifice. He married his brother's wife, and through her influence, seized John and put him in prison, intending however to release him. While there confined, John heard through his disciples of the mighty works of Jesus. He could not listen to His gracious words; but the disciples informed him and comforted him with what they had heard. Soon John was beheaded, through the influence of Herod's wife. I saw that the humblest disciples who followed Jesus, witnessed His miracles, and heard the comforting words which fell from His lips, were greater than John the Baptist; that is, they were more exalted and honored, and had more pleasure in their lives.

John came in the spirit and power of Elijah to proclaim the first advent of Jesus. I was pointed down to the last days and saw that John represented those who should go forth in the spirit and power of Elijah to herald the day of wrath and the second advent of Jesus.

After the baptism of Jesus in Jordan, He was led by the Spirit into the wilderness, to be tempted of the devil. The Holy Spirit had prepared Him for that special scene of fierce temptations. Forty days He was tempted of Satan, and in those days He ate nothing. Everything around Him was unpleasant, from which human nature would be led to shrink. He was with the wild beasts and the devil, in a desolate, lonely place. The Son of God was pale and emaciated, through fasting and suffering. But His course was marked out, and He must fulfill the work which He came to do.

Satan took advantage of the sufferings of the Son of God and prepared to beset Him with manifold temptations, hoping to obtain the victory over Him, because He had humbled Himself as a man. Satan came with this temptation: "If Thou be the Son of God, command this stone that it be made bread." He tempted Jesus to condescend to give him proof of His being the Messiah, by exercising His divine power. Jesus mildly answered him, "It is written, That man shall not live by bread alone, but by every word of God."

Satan was seeking a dispute with Jesus concerning His being the Son of God. He referred to His weak, suffering condition and boastingly affirmed that he was stronger than Jesus. But the word spoken from heaven, "Thou art My beloved Son; in Thee I am well pleased," was sufficient to sustain Jesus through all His sufferings. I saw that Christ had nothing to do in convincing Satan of His power or of His being the Saviour of the world. Satan had sufficient evidence of the exalted station and authority of the Son of God. His unwillingness to yield to Christ's authority had shut him out of heaven.

Satan, to manifest his power, carried Jesus to Jerusalem, and set Him upon a pinnacle of the temple, and there tempted Him to give evidence that He was the Son of God, by casting Himself down from that dizzy height. Satan came with the words of inspiration: "For it is written, He shall give His angels charge over Thee, to keep Thee: and in their hands they shall bear Thee up, lest at any time Thou dash Thy foot against a stone." Jesus answering said unto him, "It is said, Thou shalt not tempt the Lord thy God." Satan wished to cause Jesus to presume upon the mercy of His Father and risk His life before the fulfillment of His mission. He had hoped that the plan of salvation would fail; but the plan was laid too deep to be overthrown or marred by Satan.

Christ is the example for all Christians. When they are tempted, or their rights are disputed, they should bear it patiently. They should not feel that they have a right to call upon the Lord to display His power that they may obtain a victory over their enemies, unless God can be directly honored and glorified thereby. If Jesus had cast Himself from the pinnacle of the temple, it would not have glorified His Father; for none would have witnessed the act but Satan and the angels of God. And it would have been tempting the Lord to display His power to His bitterest foe. It would have been condescending to the one whom Jesus came to conquer.

"And the devil, taking Him up into an high mountain, showed unto Him all the kingdoms of the world in a moment of time. And the devil said unto Him, All this power will I give Thee, and the glory of them: for that is delivered unto me; and to whomsoever I will I give it. If Thou therefore wilt worship me, all shall be Thine. And Jesus answered and said unto him, Get thee behind Me, Satan: for it is written, Thou shalt worship the Lord thy God, and Him only shalt thou serve."

Satan presented before Jesus the kingdoms of the world in the most attractive light. If Jesus would there worship him, he offered to relinquish his claims to the possessions of earth. If the plan of salvation should be carried out, and Jesus should die to redeem man, Satan knew that his own power must be limited and finally taken away, and that he would be destroyed. Therefore it was his studied plan to prevent, if possible, the completion of the great work which had been commenced by the Son of God. If the plan of man's redemption should fail, Satan would retain the kingdom which he then claimed. And if he should succeed, he flattered himself that he would reign in opposition to the God of heaven.

Satan exulted when Jesus laid aside His power and glory and left heaven. He thought that the Son of God was then placed in his power. The temptation took so easily with the holy pair in Eden that he hoped by his satanic power and cunning to overthrow even the Son of God, and thereby save his own life and kingdom. If he could tempt Jesus to depart from the will of His Father, his object would be gained. But Jesus met the tempter with the rebuke, "Get thee behind Me, Satan." He was to bow only to His Father. Satan claimed the kingdom of earth as his and insinuated to Jesus that all His sufferings might be saved: that He need not die to obtain the kingdoms of this world; if He would worship him He might have all the possessions of earth and the glory of reigning over them. But Jesus was steadfast. He knew that the time was to come when He would by His own life redeem the kingdom from Satan, and that, after a season, all in heaven and earth would submit to Him. He chose His life of suffering and His dreadful death, as the way appointed by His Father that He might become a lawful heir to the kingdoms of earth and have them given into His hands as an everlasting possession. Satan also will be given into His hands to be destroyed by death, nevermore to annoy Jesus or the saints in glory.

6

The Ministry of Christ

After Satan had ended his temptations, he departed from Jesus for a season, and angels prepared Him food in the wilderness, and strengthened Him, and the blessing of His Father rested upon Him. Satan had failed in his fiercest temptations; yet he looked forward to the period of Jesus' ministry, when he should at different times try his cunning against Him. He still hoped to prevail against Him by stirring up those who would not receive Jesus, to hate and seek to destroy Him.

Satan held a special council with his angels. They were disappointed and enraged that they had prevailed nothing against the Son of God. They decided that they must be more cunning and use their power to the utmost to inspire unbelief in the minds of His own nation as to His being the Saviour of the world, and in this way discourage Jesus in His mission. No matter how exact the Jews might be in their ceremonies and sacrifices, if they could be kept blinded as to the prophecies and be made to believe that the Messiah was to appear as a mighty worldly king, they might be led to despise and reject Jesus.

I was shown that Satan and his angels were very busy during Christ's ministry, inspiring men with unbelief, hate, and scorn. Often when Jesus uttered some cutting truth, reproving their sins, the people would become enraged. Satan and his angels urged them on to take the life of the Son of God. More than once they took up stones to cast at Him, but angels guarded Him and bore Him away from the angry multitude to a place of safety. Again, as the plain truth dropped from His holy lips, the multitude laid hold of Him and led Him to the brow of a hill, intending to cast Him down. A contention arose among themselves as to what they should do with Him, when the angels again hid Him from the sight of the multitude, and He, passing through the midst of them, went His way.

Satan still hoped that the great plan of salvation would fail. He exerted all his power to make the hearts of the people hard and their feelings bitter against Jesus. He hoped that so few would receive Him as the Son of God that He would consider His sufferings and sacrifice too great to make for so small a company. But I saw that if there had been but two who would have accepted Jesus as the Son of God and believed on Him to the saving of their souls, He would have carried out the plan.

Jesus began His work by breaking Satan's power over the suffering. He restored the sick to health, gave sight to the blind, and healed the lame, causing them to leap for joy and to glorify God. He restored to health those who had been infirm and bound by Satan's cruel power many years. With gracious words He comforted the weak, the trembling, and the desponding. The feeble, suffering ones whom Satan held in triumph, Jesus wrenched from his grasp, bringing to them soundness of body and great joy and happiness. He raised the dead to life, and they glorified God for the mighty display of His power. He wrought mightily for all who believed on Him.

The life of Christ was filled with words and acts of benevolence, sympathy, and love. He was ever attentive to listen to and relieve the woes of those who came to Him. Multitudes carried in their own persons the evidence of His divine power. Yet after the work had been accomplished, many were ashamed of the humble yet mighty teacher. Because the rulers did not believe on Him, the people were not willing to accept Jesus. He was a man of sorrows and acquainted with grief. They could not endure to be governed by His sober, self-denying life. They wished to enjoy the honor which the world bestows. Yet many followed the Son of God and listened to His instructions, feasting upon the words which fell so graciously from His lips. His words were full of meaning, yet so plain that the weakest could understand them.

Satan and his angels blinded the eyes and darkened the understanding of the Jews, and stirred up the chief of the people and the rulers to take the Saviour's life. Others were sent to bring Jesus unto them; but as they came near where He was they were greatly amazed. They saw Him filled with sympathy and compassion, as He witnessed human woe. They heard Him in love and tenderness speak encouragingly to the weak and afflicted. They also heard Him, in a voice of authority, rebuke the power of Satan and bid his captives go free. They listened to the words of wisdom that fell from His lips, and they were captivated; they could not lay hands on Him. They returned to the priests and elders without Jesus.

When asked, "Why have ye not brought Him?" they related what they had witnessed of His miracles, and the holy words of wisdom, love, and knowledge which they had heard, and ended with saying, "Never man spake like this man." The chief priests accused them of being also deceived, and some of the officers were ashamed that they had not taken Him. The priests inquired in a scornful manner if any of the rulers had believed on Him. I saw that many of the magistrates and elders did believe on Jesus; but Satan kept them from acknowledging it; they feared the reproach of the people more than they feared God.

Thus far the cunning and hatred of Satan had not broken up the plan of salvation. The time for the accomplishment of the object for which Jesus came into the world was drawing near. Satan and his angels consulted together and decided to inspire Christ's own nation to cry eagerly for His blood and heap upon Him cruelty and scorn. They hoped that Jesus would resent such treatment and fail to maintain His humility and meekness.

While Satan was laying his plans, Jesus was carefully

opening to His disciples the sufferings through which He must pass—that He would be crucified and that He would rise again the third day. But their understanding seemed dull, and they could not comprehend what He told them.

The faith of the disciples was greatly strengthened at the transfiguration, when they were permitted to behold Christ's glory and to hear the voice from heaven testifying to His divine character. God chose to give the followers of Jesus strong proof that He was the promised Messiah, that in their bitter sorrow and disappointment at His crucifixion, they would not entirely cast away their confidence. At the transfiguration the Lord sent Moses and Elijah to talk with Jesus concerning His sufferings and death. Instead of choosing angels to converse with His Son, God chose those who had themselves experienced the trials of earth.

Elijah had walked with God. His work had been painful and trying, for the Lord through him had reproved the sins of Israel. Elijah was a prophet of God; yet he was compelled to flee from place to place to save his life. His own nation hunted him like a wild beast that they might destroy him. But God translated Elijah. Angels bore him in glory and triumph to heaven.

Moses was greater than any who had lived before him. He had been highly honored of God, being privileged to talk with the Lord face to face, as a man speaks with a friend. He was permitted to see the bright light and excellent glory that enshrouded the Father. The Lord through Moses delivered the children of Israel from Egyptian bondage. Moses was a mediator for his people, often standing between them and the wrath of God. When the anger of the Lord was greatly kindled against Israel for their unbelief, their murmurings, and their grievous sins, Moses' love for them was tested. God proposed to destroy them and to make of him a mighty nation. Moses showed his love for Israel by his earnest pleading in their behalf. In his distress he prayed God to turn from His fierce anger and forgive Israel, or blot his name out of His book.

Moses passed through death, but Michael came down and gave him life before his body had seen corruption. Satan tried to hold the body, claiming it as his; but Michael resurrected Moses and took him to heaven. Satan railed bitterly against God, denouncing Him as unjust in permitting his prey to be taken from him; but Christ did not rebuke His adversary, though it was through his temptation that the servant of God had fallen. He meekly referred him to His Father, saying, "The Lord rebuke thee."

Jesus had told His disciples that there were some standing with Him who should not taste of death till they should see the kingdom of God come with power. At the transfiguration this promise was fulfilled. The countenance of Jesus was there changed and shone like the sun. His raiment was white and glistening. Moses was present to represent those who will be raised from the dead at the second appearing of Jesus. And Elijah, who was translated without seeing death, represented those who will be changed to immortality at Christ's second coming and will be translated to heaven without seeing death. The disciples beheld with astonishment and fear the excellent majesty of Jesus and the cloud that overshadowed them, and heard the voice of God in terrible majesty, saying, "This is My beloved Son; hear Him."

7

The Betrayal of Christ

I was carried down to the time when Jesus ate the Passover supper with His disciples. Satan had deceived Judas and led him to think that he was one of Christ's true disciples; but his heart had ever been carnal. He had seen the mighty works of Jesus, he had been with Him through His ministry, and had yielded to the overpowering evidence that He was the Messiah; but Judas was close and covetous; he loved money. He complained in anger of the costly ointment poured upon Jesus. Mary loved her Lord. He had forgiven her sins, which were many, and had raised from the dead her much-loved brother, and she felt that nothing was too dear to bestow upon Jesus. The more precious the ointment, the better could she express her gratitude to her Saviour by devoting it to Him. Judas, as an excuse for his covetousness, urged that the ointment might have been sold and given to the poor. But it was not because he had any care for the poor; for he was selfish, and often appropriated to his own use that which was entrusted to his care to be given unto the poor. Judas had been inattentive to the comfort and even to the wants of Jesus, and to excuse his covetousness he often referred to the poor. This act of generosity on the part of Mary was a most cutting rebuke of his covetous disposition. The way was prepared for Satan's temptation to find a ready reception in the heart of Judas.

The priests and rulers of the Jews hated Jesus; but multitudes thronged to listen to His words of wisdom and to witness His mighty works. The people were stirred with the deepest interest and anxiously followed Jesus to hear the instructions of this wonderful teacher. Many of the rulers believed on Him, but dared not confess their faith lest they should be put out of the synagogue. The priests and elders decided that something must be done to draw the attention of the people from Jesus. They feared that all men would believe on Him. They could see no safety for themselves. They must lose their position or put Jesus to death. And after they should put Him to death, there would still be those who were living monuments of His power. Jesus had raised Lazarus from the dead, and they feared that if they should kill Jesus, Lazarus would testify of His mighty power. The people were flocking to see him who was raised from the dead, and the rulers determined to slay Lazarus also, and put down the excitement. Then they would turn the people to the traditions and doctrines of men, to tithe mint and rue, and again have influence over them. They agreed to take Jesus when He was alone; for if they should attempt to take Him in a crowd, when the minds of the people were all interested in Him, they would be stoned.

Judas knew how anxious they were to obtain Jesus and offered to betray Him to the chief priests and elders for a few pieces of silver. His love of money led him to agree to betray his Lord into the hands of His bitterest enemies. Satan was working directly through Judas, and in the midst of the impressive scene of the last supper, the traitor was devising plans to betray his Master. Jesus sorrowfully told His disciples that all of them would be offended because of Him that night. But Peter ardently affirmed that although all others should be offended because of Him, he would not be offended. Jesus said to Peter: "Satan hath desired to have you, that he may sift you as wheat: but I have prayed for thee, that thy faith fail not: and when thou art converted, strengthen thy brethren." Luke 22:31,32.

I beheld Jesus in the garden with His disciples. In deep sorrow He bade them watch and pray, lest they should enter into temptation. He knew that their faith was to be tried, and their hopes disappointed, and that they would need all the strength which they could obtain by close watching and fervent prayer. With strong cries and weeping, Jesus prayed, "Father, if Thou be willing, remove this cup from Me: nevertheless not My will, but Thine, be done." The Son of God prayed in agony. Great drops of blood gathered upon His face and fell to the ground. Angels were hovering over the place, witnessing the scene, but only one was commissioned to go and strengthen the Son of God in His agony. There was no joy in heaven. The angels cast their crowns and harps from them and with the deepest interest silently watched Jesus. They wished to surround the Son of God, but the commanding angels suffered them not, lest, as they should behold His betrayal, they should deliver Him; for the plan had been laid, and it must be fulfilled.

After Jesus had prayed, He came to His disciples; but they were sleeping. In that dreadful hour He had not the sympathy and prayers of even His disciples. Peter, who was so zealous a short time before, was heavy with sleep. Jesus reminded him of his positive declarations and said to him, "What, could ye not watch with Me one hour?" Three times the Son of God prayed in agony. Then Judas, with his band of armed men, appeared. He approached his Master as usual, to salute Him. The band surrounded Jesus; but there He manifested His divine power, as He said, "Whom seek ye?" "I am He." They fell backward to the ground. Jesus made this inquiry that they might witness His power and have evidence that He could deliver Himself from their hands if He would.

The disciples began to hope as they saw the multitude with their staves and swords fall so quickly. As they arose and again surrounded the Son of God, Peter drew his sword and smote a servant of the high priest and cut off an ear. Jesus bade him to put up the sword, saying, "Thinkest thou that I cannot now pray to My Father, and He shall presently give Me more than twelve legions of angels?" I saw that as these words were spoken, the countenances of the angels were animated with hope. They wished then and there to surround their Commander and disperse that angry mob. But again sadness settled upon them, as Jesus added, "But how then shall the Scriptures be fulfilled, that thus it must be?" The hearts of the disciples also sank in despair and bitter disappointment, as Jesus suffered Himself to be led away by His enemies.

The disciples feared for their own lives, and they all forsook Him and fled. Jesus was left alone in the hands of the murderous mob. Oh, what a triumph of Satan then! And what sadness and sorrow with the angels of God! Many companies of holy angels, each with a tall commanding angel at their head, were sent to witness the scene. They were to record every insult and cruelty imposed upon the Son of God, and to register every pang of anguish which Jesus should suffer; for the very men who joined in this dreadful scene are to see it all again in living characters.

8

The Trial of Christ

T he angels as they left heaven, in sadness laid off their glittering crowns. They could not wear them while their Commander was suffering and was to wear a crown of thorns. Satan and his angels were busy in the judgment hall to destroy human feeling and sympathy. The very atmosphere was heavy and polluted by their influence. The chief priests and elders were inspired by them to insult and abuse Jesus in a manner the most difficult for human nature to bear. Satan hoped that such mockery and violence would call forth from the Son of God some complaint or murmur; or that He would manifest His divine power, and wrench Himself from the grasp of the multitude, and that thus the plan of salvation might at last fail.

Peter followed his Lord after His betrayal. He was anxious to see what would be done with Jesus. But when he was accused of being one of His disciples, fear for his own safety led him to declare that he knew not the man. The disciples were noted for the purity of their language, and Peter, to convince his accusers that he was not one of Christ's disciples, denied the charge the third time with cursing and swearing. Jesus, who was at some distance from Peter, turned a sorrowful reproving gaze upon him. Then the disciple remembered the words which Jesus had spoken to him in the upper chamber, and also his own zealous assertion, "Though all men shall be offended because of Thee, yet will I never be offended." He had denied his Lord, even with cursing and swearing; but that look of

Jesus' melted Peter's heart and saved him. He wept bitterly and repented of his great sin, and was converted, and then was prepared to strengthen his brethren.

The multitude were clamorous for the blood of Jesus. They cruelly scourged Him, and put upon Him an old purple kingly robe, and bound His sacred head with a crown of thorns. They put a reed into His hand, and bowed to Him, and mockingly saluted Him, "Hail, king of the Jews!" They then took the reed from His hand and smote Him with it upon the head, causing the thorns to penetrate His temples, sending the blood trickling down His face and beard.

It was difficult for the angels to endure the sight. They would have delivered Jesus, but the commanding angels forbade them, saying that it was a great ransom which was to be paid for man; but it would be complete and would cause the death of him who had the power of death. Jesus knew that angels were witnessing the scene of His humiliation. The weakest angel could have caused that mocking throng to fall powerless and could have delivered Jesus. He knew that if He should desire it of His Father, angels would instantly release Him. But it was necessary that He should suffer the violence of wicked men, in order to carry out the plan of salvation.

Jesus stood meek and humble before the infuriated multitude, while they offered Him the vilest abuse. They spit in His face—that face from which they will one day desire to hide, which will give light to the city of God and shine brighter than the sun. Christ did not cast upon the offenders an angry look. They covered His head with an old garment, blindfolding Him, and then struck Him in the face and cried out, "Prophesy, who is it that smote Thee?" There was commotion among the angels. They would have rescued Him instantly; but their commanding angels restrained them.

Some of the disciples had gained confidence to enter where Jesus was and witness His trial. They expected that He would manifest His divine power, and deliver Himself from the hands of His enemies, and punish them for their cruelty toward Him.

Their hopes would rise and fall as the different scenes tran-
spired. Sometimes they doubted, and feared that they had been
deceived. But the voice heard at the mount of transfiguration,
and the glory they there beheld, strengthened their faith that
He was the Son of God. They called to mind the scenes which
they had witnessed, the miracles which they had seen Jesus
perform in healing the sick, opening the eyes of the blind, un-
stopping the deaf ears, rebuking and casting out devils, raising
the dead to life, and even calming the wind and the sea. They
could not believe that He would die. They hoped that He would
yet rise in power, and with His commanding voice disperse that
bloodthirsty multitude, as when He entered the temple and
drove out those who were making the house of God a place of
merchandise, when they fled before Him as if pursued by a
company of armed soldiers. The disciples hoped that Jesus
would manifest His power and convince all that He was the
King of Israel.

Judas was filled with bitter remorse and shame at his treach-
erous act in betraying Jesus. And when he witnessed the abuse
which the Saviour endured, he was overcome. He had loved
Jesus, but had loved money more. He had not thought that Jesus
would suffer Himself to be taken by the mob which he led on.
He had expected Him to work a miracle, and deliver Himself
from them. But when he saw the infuriated multitude in the
judgment hall, thirsting for blood, he deeply felt his guilt; and
while many were vehemently accusing Jesus, Judas rushed
through the multitude, confessing that he had sinned in betraying innocent blood. He offered the priests the money which
they had paid him, and entreated them to release Jesus, declar-
ing that He was entirely innocent.

For a short time vexation and confusion kept the priests
silent. They did not wish the people to know that they had hired
one of the professed followers of Jesus to betray Him into their
hands. Their hunting Jesus like a thief and taking Him secretly,
they wished to hide. But the confession of Judas, and his
haggard, guilty appearance, exposed the priests before the

multitude, showing that it was hatred that had caused them to take Jesus. As Judas loudly declared Jesus to be innocent, the priests replied, "What is that to us? see thou to that." They had Jesus in their power, and were determined to make sure of Him. Judas, overwhelmed with anguish, threw the money that he now despised at the feet of those who had hired him, and, in anguish and horror, went and hanged himself.

Jesus had many sympathizers in the company about Him, and His answering nothing to the many questions put to Him amazed the throng. Under all the mockery and violence of the mob, not a frown, not a troubled expression, rested upon His features. He was dignified and composed. The spectators looked upon Him with wonder. They compared His perfect form and firm, dignified bearing with the appearance of those who sat in judgment against Him, and said to one another that He appeared more like a king than any of the rulers. He bore no marks of being a criminal. His eye was mild, clear, and undaunted, His forehead broad and high. Every feature was strongly marked with benevolence and noble principle. His patience and forbearance were so unlike man that many trembled. Even Herod and Pilate were greatly troubled at His noble, Godlike bearing.

From the first, Pilate was convicted that Jesus was no common man. He believed Him to be an excellent character, and entirely innocent of the charges brought against Him. The angels who were witnessing the scene marked the convictions of the Roman governor, and to save him from engaging in the awful act of delivering Christ to be crucified, an angel was sent to Pilate's wife, and gave her information through a dream that it was the Son of God in whose trial her husband was engaged, and that He was an innocent sufferer. She immediately sent a message to Pilate, stating that she had suffered many things in a dream on account of Jesus and warning him to have nothing to do with that holy man. The messenger, pressing hastily through the crowd, placed the letter in the hands of Pilate. As he read, he trembled and turned pale, and at once determined to have nothing to do with putting Christ to death. If the Jews would have the blood of Jesus, he would not give his influence to it, but would labor to deliver Him.

When Pilate heard that Herod was in Jerusalem, he was greatly relieved; for he hoped to free himself from all responsibility in the trial and condemnation of Jesus. He at once sent Him, with His accusers, to Herod. This ruler had become hardened in sin. The murder of John the Baptist had left upon his conscience a stain from which he could not free himself. When he heard of Jesus and the mighty works wrought by Him, he feared and trembled, believing Him to be John the Baptist risen from the dead. When Jesus was placed in his hands by Pilate, Herod considered the act an acknowledgment of his power, authority, and judgment. This had the effect to make friends of the two rulers, who had before been enemies. Herod was pleased to see Jesus, expecting Him to work some mighty miracle for his satisfaction. But it was not the work of Jesus to gratify curiosity or to seek His own safety. His divine, miraculous power was to be exercised for the salvation of others, but not in His own behalf.

Jesus answered nothing to the many questions put to Him by Herod; neither did He reply to His enemies, who were vehemently accusing Him. Herod was enraged because Jesus did not appear to fear his power, and with his men of war he derided, mocked, and abused the Son of God. Yet he was astonished at the noble, Godlike appearance of Jesus when shamefully abused, and fearing to condemn Him, he sent Him again to Pilate.

Satan and his angels were tempting Pilate and trying to lead him on to his own ruin. They suggested to him that if he did not take part in condemning Jesus others would; the multitude were thirsting for His blood; and if he did not deliver Him to be crucified, he would lose his power and worldly honor and would be denounced as a believer on the impostor. Through fear of losing his power and authority, Pilate consented to the death of Jesus. And notwithstanding he placed the blood of Jesus upon His accusers, and the multitude received it, crying,

"His blood be on us, and on our children," yet Pilate was not clear; he was guilty of the blood of Christ. For his own selfish interest, his love of honor from the great men of earth, he delivered an innocent man to die. If Pilate had followed his own convictions, he would have had nothing to do with condemning Jesus.

The appearance and words of Jesus during His trial made a deep impression upon the minds of many who were present on that occasion. The result of the influence thus exerted was apparent after His resurrection. Among those who were then added to the church, there were many whose conviction dated from the time of Jesus' trial.

Satan's rage was great as he saw that all the cruelty which he had led the Jews to inflict on Jesus had not called forth from Him the slightest murmur. Although He had taken upon Himself man's nature, He was sustained by a Godlike fortitude, and departed not in the least from the will of His Father.

9

Amazing Love

Christ, the precious Son of God, was led forth and delivered to the people to be crucified. The disciples and believers from the region round about joined the throng that followed Jesus to Calvary. The mother of Jesus was also there, supported by John, the beloved disciple. Her heart was stricken with unutterable anguish; yet she, with the disciples, hoped that the painful scene would change, and Jesus would assert his power, and appear before his enemies as the Son of God. Then again her mother's heart would sink as she remembered words in which he had briefly referred to the things which were that day being enacted.

Jesus had scarcely passed the gate of Pilate's house when the cross which had been prepared for Barabbas was brought out and laid upon his bruised and bleeding shoulders. Crosses were also placed upon the companions of Barabbas, who were to suffer death at the same time with Jesus. The Saviour had borne his burden but a few rods, when, from loss of blood and excessive weariness and pain, he fell fainting to the ground.

When Jesus revived, the cross was again placed upon his shoulders and he was forced forward. He staggered on for a few steps, bearing his heavy load, then fell as one lifeless to the ground. He was at first pronounced to be dead, but finally he again revived. The priests and rulers felt no compassion for their suffering victim; but they saw that it was impossible for him to carry the instrument of torture farther.

While they were considering what to do, Simon, a Cyrenian, coming from an opposite direction, met the crowd, was seized at the instigation of the priests, and compelled to carry the cross of Christ. The sons of Simon were disciples of Jesus, but he himself had never been connected with Him.

A great multitude followed the Saviour to Calvary, many mocking and deriding; but some were weeping and recounting his praise. Those whom he had healed of various infirmities, and those whom he had raised from the dead, declared his marvelous works with earnest voice, and demanded to know what Jesus had done that he should be treated as a malefactor. Only a few days before, they had attended him with joyful hosannas, and the waving of palm-branches, as he rode triumphantly to Jerusalem. But many who had then shouted his praise, because it was popular to do so, now swelled the cry of "Crucify him! Crucify him!"

Upon arriving at the place of execution, the condemned were bound to the instruments of torture. While the two thieves wrestled in the hands of those who stretched them upon the cross, Jesus made no resistance. The mother of Jesus looked on with agonizing suspense, hoping that He would work a miracle to save Himself. She saw his hands stretched upon the cross—those dear hands that had ever dispensed blessings, and had been reached forth so many times to heal the suffering. And now the hammer and nails were brought, and as the spikes were driven through the tender flesh and fastened to the cross, the heart-stricken disciples bore away from the cruel scene the fainting form of the mother of Christ.

Jesus made no murmur of complaint; his face remained pale and serene, but great drops of sweat stood upon his brow. There was no pitying hand to wipe the death-dew from His face, nor words of sympathy and unchanging fidelity to stay His human heart. He was treading the wine-press all alone; and of all the people there was none with Him. While the soldiers were doing their fearful work, and He was enduring the most acute agony, Jesus prayed for His enemies—"Father, forgive them;

for they know not what they do." That prayer of Christ for his enemies embraced the world, taking in every sinner who should live, until the end of time.

After Jesus was nailed to the cross, it was lifted by several powerful men, and thrust with great violence into the place prepared for it, causing the most excruciating agony to the Son of God. And now a terrible scene was enacted. Priests, rulers, and scribes forgot the dignity of their sacred offices, and joined with the rabble in mocking and jeering the dying Son of God, saying, "If Thou be the King of the Jews, save Thyself." And some deridingly repeated among themselves: "He saved others; himself he cannot save. The dignitaries of the temple, the hardened soldiers, the vile thief upon the cross, and the base and cruel among the multitude, all united in their abuse of Christ.

The thieves who were crucified with Jesus suffered like physical torture with him; but one was only hardened and rendered desperate and defiant by his pain. He took up the mocking of the priests, and railed upon Jesus, saying, "If thou be Christ, save thyself and us." The other malefactor was not a hardened criminal; his morals had been corrupted by association with the base, but his crimes were not so great as were those of many who stood beneath the cross reviling the Saviour. When he heard the sneering words of his companion in crime, he "rebuked him, saying, Dost thou not fear God, seeing thou art in the same condemnation? And we indeed justly; for we receive the due reward of our deeds; but this man hath done nothing amiss." Then, as his heart went out to Christ, heavenly illumination flooded his mind. In Jesus, bruised, mocked, and hanging upon the cross, he saw his Redeemer, his only hope, and appealed to him in humble faith: "Lord, remember me when thou comest into thy kingdom! And Jesus said unto him, Verily I say unto thee to-day,* shalt thou be with me

---

*By placing the coma after the word *to-day*, instead of after the word *thee*, as in the common versions, the true meaning of the text is more apparent.

in Paradise."

With amazement the angels beheld the infinite love of Jesus, who, suffering the most excruciating agony of mind and body, thought only of others, and encouraged the penitent soul to believe. While pouring out his life in death, He exercised a love for man stronger than death. Many who witnessed those scenes upon Calvary were afterward established by them in the faith of Christ.

The enemies of Jesus now awaited his death with impatient hope. That event they imagined would forever hush the rumors of his divine power, and the wonders of his miracles. They flattered themselves that they should then no longer tremble because of his influence. The unfeeling soldiers who had stretched the body of Jesus upon the cross, divided his clothing among themselves, contending over one garment, which was woven without seam. They finally decided the matter by casting lots for it. The pen of inspiration had accurately described this scene hundreds of years before it took place: "For dogs have compassed me; the assembly of the wicked have inclosed me; they pierced my hands and my feet." "They parted my raiment among them, and for my vesture they did cast lots."

The eyes of Jesus wandered over the multitude that had collected together to witness his death, and he saw at the foot of the cross John supporting Mary, the mother of Christ. She had returned to the terrible scene, not being able to longer remain away from her Son. The last lesson of Jesus was one of filial love. He looked upon the grief-stricken face of his mother, and then upon John; said He, addressing the former: "Woman, behold thy son." Then, to the disciple: "Behold, thy mother," John well understood the words of Jesus, and the sacred trust which was committed to him. He immediately removed the mother of Christ from the fearful scene of Calvary. From that hour he cared for her as would a dutiful son, taking her to his own home. The perfect example of Christ's filial love shines forth with undimmed luster from the mist of ages. While enduring the keenest torture, he was not forgetful of his mother, but made all provision necessary for her future.

The mission of Christ's earthly life was now nearly accomplished. His tongue was parched, and he said, "I thirst." They saturated a sponge with vinegar and gall and offered it him to drink; and when he had tasted it, he refused it. And now the Lord of life and glory was dying, a ransom for the race. It was the sense of sin, bringing the Father's wrath upon him as man's substitute, that made the cup he drank so bitter, and broke the heart of the Son of God.

As man's substitute and surety, the iniquity of men was laid upon Christ; he was counted a transgressor that he might redeem them from the curse of the law. The guilt of every descendant of Adam of every age was pressing upon his heart; and the wrath of God, and the terrible manifestation of his displeasure because of iniquity, filled the soul of his Son with consternation. The withdrawal of the divine countenance from the Saviour, in this hour of supreme anguish, pierced his heart with a sorrow that can never be fully understood by man. Every pang endured by the Son of God upon the cross, the blood drops that flowed from his head, his hands, and feet, the convulsions of agony which racked his frame, and the unutterable anguish that filled his soul at the hiding of his Father's face from him, speak to man, saying, It is for love of thee that the Son of God consents to have these heinous crimes laid upon him; for thee he spoils the domain of death, and opens the gates of Paradise and immortal life. He who stilled the angry waves by his word, and walked the foam-capped billows, who made devils tremble, and disease flee from his touch, who raised the dead to life and opened the eyes of the blind,—offers himself upon the cross as the last sacrifice for man. He, the sin-bearer, endures judicial punishment for iniquity, and becomes sin itself for man.

Satan, with his fierce temptations, wrung the heart of Jesus. Sin, so hateful to his sight, was heaped upon him till he groaned beneath its weight. No wonder that his humanity trembled in that fearful hour. Angels witnessed with amazement the despairing agony of the Son of God, so much greater than his physical pain that the latter was hardly felt by him. The hosts of Heaven veiled their faces from the fearful sight.

Inanimate nature expressed a sympathy with its insulted and dying Author. The sun refused to look upon the awful scene. Its full, bright rays were illuminating the earth at midday, when suddenly it seemed to be blotted out. Complete darkness enveloped the cross, and all the vicinity about, like a funeral pall. The darkness lasted three full hours. At the ninth hour the terrible darkness lifted from the people, but still wrapt the Saviour as in a mantle. The angry lightnings seemed to be hurled at Him as He hung upon the cross. Then "Jesus cried with a loud voice, saying, Eloi, eloi, lama sabacthani? which is, being interpreted, My God, my God, why hast thou forsaken me?"

In silence the people watch for the end of this fearful scene. Again the sun shines forth; but the cross is enveloped in darkness. Priests and rulers look toward Jerusalem; and lo, the dense cloud has settled upon the city, and over Judah's plains, and the fierce lightnings of God's wrath are directed against the fated city. Suddenly the gloom is lifted from the cross, and in clear trumpet tones, that seem to resound throughout creation, Jesus cries, "It is finished;" "Father, into thy hands I commend my spirit." A light encircled the cross, and the face of the Saviour shone with a glory like unto the sun. He then bowed his head upon his breast, and died.

At the moment in which Christ died, there were priests ministering in the temple before the vail which separated the holy from the most holy place. Suddenly they felt the earth tremble beneath them, and the vail of the temple, a strong, rich drapery that had been renewed yearly, was rent in twain from top to bottom by the same bloodless hand that wrote the words of doom upon the walls of Belshazzar's palace.

Jesus did not yield up his life till he had accomplished the work which he came to do; and he exclaimed with his parting breath, "It is finished!" Angels rejoiced as the words were uttered; for the great plan of redemption was being triumphantly carried out. There was joy in Heaven that the sons of Adam could now, through a life of obedience, be exalted finally to the presence of God. Satan was defeated, and knew that his kingdom was lost.

John was at a loss to know what measures he should take in regard to the body of his beloved Master. He shuddered at the thought of its being handled by rough and unfeeling soldiers, and placed in a dishonored burial place. He knew he could obtain no favors from the Jewish authorities, and he could hope little from Pilate. But Joseph and Nicodemus came to the front in this emergency. Both of these men were members of the Sanhedrin, and acquainted with Pilate. Both were men of wealth and influence. They were determined that the body of Jesus should have an honorable burial.

Joseph went boldly to Pilate, and begged from him the body of Jesus for burial. Pilate then gave an official order that the body of Jesus should be given to Joseph. While the disciple John was anxious and troubled about the sacred remains of his beloved Master, Joseph of Arimathea returned with the commission from the governor; and Nicodemus, anticipating the result of Joseph's interview with Pilate, came with a costly mixture of myrrh and aloes of about one hundred pounds' weight. The most honored in all Jerusalem could not have been shown more respect in death.

Gently and reverently they removed with their own hands the body of Jesus from the instrument of torture, their sympathetic tears falling fast as they looked upon his bruised and lacerated form, which they carefully bathed and cleansed from the stain of blood. Joseph owned a new tomb, hewn from stone, which he was reserving for himself; it was near Calvary, and he now prepared this sepulcher for Jesus. The body, together with the spices brought by Nicodemus, was carefully wrapped in a linen sheet, and the three disciples bore their precious burden to the new sepulcher, wherein man had never before lain. There they straightened those mangled limbs, and folded the bruised hands upon the pulseless breast. The Galilean women drew near, to see that all had been done that could be done for the lifeless form of their beloved Teacher. Then they saw the heavy stone rolled against the entrance of the sepulcher, and the Son of God was left at rest. The women were last at the cross, and last at the tomb of Christ.

Although the Jewish rulers had carried out their fiendish purpose in putting to death the Son of God, their apprehensions were not quieted, nor was their jealousy of Christ dead. Mingled with the joy of gratified revenge, there was an ever-present fear that his dead body lying in Joseph's tomb would come forth to life. Therefore "the chief priests and Pharisees came together unto Pilate, saying, Sir, we remember that that deceiver said, while he was yet alive, After three days I will rise again. Command, therefore, that the sepulcher be made sure until the third day, lest his disciples come by night, and steal him away, and say unto the people, He is risen from the dead; so the last error shall be worse than the first." Pilate was as unwilling as were the Jews that Jesus should rise with power to punish the guilt of those who had destroyed him, and he placed a band of Roman soldiers at the command of the priests. Said he, "Ye have a watch; go your way, make it as sure as ye can. So they went, and made the sepulcher sure, sealing the stone and setting a watch."

The Jews realized the advantage of having such a guard about the tomb of Jesus. They placed a seal upon the stone that closed the sepulcher, that it might not be disturbed without the fact being known, and took every precaution against the disciples practicing any deception in regard to the body of Jesus. But all their plans and precautions only served to make the triumph of the resurrection more complete, and to more fully establish its truth.

10

The Resurrection of Christ

The disciples rested on the Sabbath, sorrowing for the death of their Lord, while Jesus, the King of glory, lay in the tomb. As night drew on, soldiers were stationed to guard the Saviour's resting place, while angels, unseen, hovered above the sacred spot. The night wore slowly away, and while it was yet dark, the watching angels knew that the time for the release of God's dear Son. their loved Commander, had nearly come. As they were waiting with the deepest emotion the hour of His triumph, a mighty angel came flying swiftly from heaven. His face was like the lightning, and his garments white as snow. His light dispersed the darkness from his track and caused the evil angels, who had triumphantly claimed the body of Jesus, to flee in terror from his brightness and glory. One of the angelic host who had witnessed the scene of Christ's humiliation, and was watching His resting place, joined the angel from heaven, and together they came down to the sepulcher. The earth trembled and shook as they approached, and there was a great earthquake.

Terror seized the Roman guard. Where was now their power to keep the body of Jesus? They did not think of their duty or of the disciples' stealing Him away. As the light of the angels shone around, brighter than the sun, that Roman guard fell as dead men to the ground. One of the angels laid hold of the great stone and rolled it away from the door of the sepulcher and seated himself upon it. The other entered the tomb and unbound the napkin from the head of Jesus.

Then the angel from heaven, with a voice that caused the earth to quake, cried out, "Thou Son of God, Thy Father calls Thee! Come forth." Death could hold dominion over Him no longer. Jesus arose from the dead, a triumphant conqueror. In solemn awe the angelic host gazed upon the scene. And as Jesus came forth from the sepulcher, those shining angels prostrated themselves to the earth in worship, and hailed Him with songs of victory and triumph.

Satan's angels had been compelled to flee before the bright, penetrating light of the heavenly angels, and they bitterly complained to their king that their prey had been violently taken from them, and that He whom they so much hated had risen from the dead. Satan and his hosts had exulted that their power over fallen man had caused the Lord of life to be laid in the grave, but short was their hellish triumph. For as Jesus walked forth from His prison house a majestic conqueror, Satan knew that after a season he must die, and his kingdom pass unto Him whose right it was. He lamented and raged that notwithstanding all his efforts, Jesus had not been overcome, but had opened a way of salvation for man, and whosoever would might walk in it and be saved.

The evil angels and their commander met in council to consider how they could still work against the government of God. Satan bade his servants go to the chief priests and elders. Said he, "We succeeded in deceiving them, blinding their eyes and hardening their hearts against Jesus. We made them believe that He was an impostor. That Roman guard will carry the hateful news that Christ has risen. We led the priests and elders on to hate Jesus and to murder Him. Now hold it before them that if it becomes known that Jesus is risen, they will be stoned by the people for putting to death an innocent man."

As the host of heavenly angels departed from the sepulcher and the light and glory passed away, the Roman guard ventured to raise their heads and look about them. They were filled with amazement as they saw that the great stone had been rolled from the door of the sepulcher and that the body of Jesus was gone. They hastened to the city to make known to the priests and elders what they had seen. As those murderers listened to the marvelous report, paleness sat upon every face. Horror seized them at the thought of what they had done. If the report was correct, they were lost. For a time they sat in silence, looking upon one another's faces, not knowing what to do or what to say. To accept the report would be to condemn themselves. They went aside to consult as to what should be done. They reasoned that if the report brought by the guard should be circulated among the people, those who put Christ to death would be slain as His murderers. It was decided to hire the soldiers to keep the matter secret. The priests and elders offered them a large sum of money, saying, "Say ye, His disciples came by night, and stole Him away while we slept." And when the guard inquired what would be done with them for sleeping at their post, the Jewish officers promised to persuade the governor and secure their safety. For the sake of money, the Roman guard sold their honor, and agreed to follow the counsel of the priests and elders.

When Jesus, as He hung upon the cross, cried out, "*It is finished,*" the rocks rent, the earth shook, and some of the graves were opened. When He arose a victor over death and the grave, while the earth was reeling and the glory of heaven shone around the sacred spot, many of the righteous dead, obedient to His call, came forth as witnesses that He had risen. Those favored, risen saints came forth glorified. They were chosen and holy ones of every age, from creation down even to the days of Christ. Thus while the Jewish leaders were seeking to conceal the fact of Christ's resurrection, God chose to bring up a company from their graves to testify that Jesus had risen, and to declare His glory.

Those risen ones differed in stature and form, some being more noble in appearance than others. I was informed that the inhabitants of earth had been degenerating, losing their strength and comeliness. Satan has the power of disease and death, and with every age the effects of the curse have been more visible, and the power of Satan more plainly seen. Those who lived in the days of Noah and Abraham resembled the angels in form, comeliness, and strength. But every succeeding generation have been growing weaker and more subject to disease, and their life has been of shorter duration. Satan has been learning how to annoy and enfeeble the race.

Those who came forth after the resurrection of Jesus appeared to many, telling them that the sacrifice for man was completed, that Jesus, whom the Jews crucified, had risen from the dead; and in proof of their words they declared, "We be risen with Him." They bore testimony that it was by His mighty power that they had been called forth from their graves. Notwithstanding the lying reports circulated, the resurrection of Christ could not be concealed by Satan, his angels, or the chief priests; for this holy company, brought forth from their graves, spread the wonderful, joyful news; also Jesus showed Himself to His sorrowing, heartbroken disciples, dispelling their fears and causing them joy and gladness.

Early in the morning of the first day of the week, before it was yet light, holy women came to the sepulcher, bringing sweet spices to anoint the body of Jesus. They found that the heavy stone had been rolled away from the door of the sepulcher, and the body of Jesus was not there. Their hearts sank within them, and they feared that their enemies had taken away the body. Suddenly they beheld two angels in white apparel, their faces bright and shining. These heavenly beings understood the errand of the women and immediately told them that Jesus was not there; He had risen, but they could behold the place where He had lain. They bade them go and tell His disciples that He would go before them into Galilee. With fear and great joy the women hurried back to the sorrowing disciples and told them the things which they had seen and heard.

The disciples could not believe that Christ had risen, but, with the women who had brought the report, ran hastily to the sepulcher. They found that Jesus was not there; they saw His linen clothes, but could not believe the good news that He had risen from the dead. They returned home marveling at what they had seen, also at the report brought them by the women. But Mary chose to linger around the sepulcher, thinking of what she had seen, and distressed with the thought that she might have been deceived. She felt that new trials awaited her. Her grief was renewed, and she broke forth in bitter weeping. She stooped down to look again into the sepulcher, and beheld two angels clothed in white. One was sitting where the head of Jesus had lain, the other where His feet had been. They spoke to her tenderly, and asked her why she wept. She replied, "They have taken away my Lord, and I know not where they have laid Him."

As she turned from the sepulcher, she saw Jesus standing near, but knew Him not. He spoke to her tenderly, inquiring the cause of her sorrow and asking whom she was seeking. Supposing that He was the gardener, she begged Him, if He had borne away her Lord, to tell her where he had laid Him, that she might take Him away. Jesus spoke to her with His own heavenly voice, saying, "Mary!" She was acquainted with the tones of that dear voice, and quickly answered, "Master!" and in her joy was about to embrace Him; but Jesus said, "Touch Me not; for I am not yet ascended to My Father: but go to My brethren, and say unto them, I ascend unto My Father, and your Father; and to My God, and your God." Joyfully she hastened to the disciples with the good news. Jesus quickly ascended to His Father to hear from His lips that He accepted the sacrifice, and to receive all power in heaven and upon earth.

Angels like a cloud surrounded the Son of God and bade the everlasting gates be lifted up, that the King of glory might come in. I saw that while Jesus was with that bright heavenly host, in the presence of God, and surrounded by His glory, He did not forget His disciples upon the earth, but received power from His Father, that He might return and impart power to them. The same day He returned and showed Himself to His disciples. He suffered them then to touch Him; for He had ascended to His Father and had received power.

At this time Thomas was not present. He would not humbly receive the report of the disciples, but firmly and self-confidently affirmed that he would not believe unless he should put his fingers in the prints of the nails and his hand in the side where the cruel spear was thrust. In this he showed a lack of confidence in his brethren. If all should require the same evidence, none would now receive Jesus and believe in His resurrection. But it was the will of God that the report of the disciples should be received by those who could not themselves see and hear the risen Saviour. God was not pleased with the unbelief of Thomas. When Jesus again met with His disciples, Thomas was with them; and when he beheld Jesus, he believed. But he had declared that he would not be satisfied without the evidence of feeling added to sight, and Jesus gave him the evidence which he had desired. Thomas cried out, "My Lord and my God!" But Jesus reproved him for his unbelief, saying, "Thomas, because thou hast seen Me, thou hast believed: blessed are they that have not seen, and yet have believed."

As the news spread from city to city and from town to town, the Jews in their turn feared for their lives and concealed the hatred which they cherished toward the disciples. Their only hope was to spread their lying report. And those who wished this lie to be true accepted it. Pilate trembled as he heard that Christ had risen. He could not doubt the testimony given, and from that hour peace left him forever. For the sake of worldly honor, for fear of losing his authority and his life, he had delivered Jesus to die. He was now fully convinced that it was not merely an innocent man of whose blood he was guilty, but the Son of God. Miserable to its close was the life of Pilate. Despair and anguish crushed every hopeful, joyful feeling. He refused to be comforted and died a most miserable death.

Jesus remained with His disciples forty days, causing them joy and gladness of heart as He opened to them more fully the realities of the kingdom of God. He commissioned them to bear testimony to the things which they had seen and heard concerning His sufferings, death, and resurrection, that He had

made a sacrifice for sin, and that all who would might come
unto Him and find life. With faithful tenderness He told them
that they would be persecuted and distressed; but they would
find relief in recalling their experience and remembering the
words which He had spoken to them. He told them that He had
overcome the temptations of Satan and obtained the victory
through trials and suffering. Satan could have no more power
over Him, but would bring his temptations to bear more directly upon them and upon all who should believe in His name.
But they could overcome as He had overcome. Jesus endowed
His disciples with power to work miracles, and told them that
although they should be persecuted by wicked men, He would
from time to time send His angels to deliver them; their lives
could not be taken until their mission should be accomplished;
then they might be required to seal with their blood the testimonies which they had borne.

His anxious followers gladly listened to His teachings, eagerly feasting upon every word which fell from His holy lips.
Now they certainly knew that He was the Saviour of the world.
His words sank deep into their hearts, and they sorrowed that
they must soon be parted from their heavenly Teacher and no
longer hear comforting, gracious words from His lips. But again
their hearts were warmed with love and exceeding joy, as Jesus
told them that He would go and prepare mansions for them and
come again and receive them, that they might be ever with Him.
He promised also to send the Comforter, the Holy Spirit, to
guide them into all truth. "And He lifted up His hands, and
blessed them."

11

The Ascension of Christ

All heaven was waiting the hour of triumph when Jesus should ascend to His Father. Angels came to receive the King of glory and to escort Him triumphantly to heaven. After Jesus had blessed His disciples, He was parted from them and taken up. And as He led the way upward, the multitude of captives who were raised at His resurrection followed. A multitude of the heavenly host were in attendance, while in heaven an innumerable company of angels awaited His coming.

As they ascended to the Holy City, the angels who escorted Jesus cried out, "Lift up your heads, O ye gates; and be ye lift up, ye everlasting doors; and the King of glory shall come in." The angels in the city cried out with rapture, "Who is this King of glory?" The escorting angels answered in triumph, "The Lord strong and mighty, the Lord mighty in battle! Lift up your heads, O ye gates; even lift them up, ye everlasting doors; and the King of glory shall come in!" Again the waiting angels asked, "Who is this King of glory?" and the escorting angels answered in melodious strains, "The Lord of hosts, He is the King of glory." And the heavenly train passed into the city of God. Then all the heavenly host surrounded their majestic Commander, and with the deepest adoration bowed before Him and cast their glittering crowns at His feet. And then they touched their golden harps, and in sweet, melodious strains filled all heaven with rich music and songs to the Lamb who was slain, yet lives again in majesty and glory.

As the disciples gazed sorrowfully toward heaven to catch the last glimpse of their ascending Lord, two angels clothed in white apparel stood by them and said to them, "Ye men of Galilee, why stand ye gazing up into heaven? this same Jesus, which is taken up from you into heaven, shall so come in like manner as ye have seen Him go into heaven." The disciples and the mother of Jesus, who with them had witnessed the ascension of the Son of God, spent the following night in talking over His wonderful acts and the strange and glorious events which had taken place within a short time.

Satan again counseled with his angels, and with bitter hatred against God's government told them that while he retained his power and authority upon earth their efforts must be tenfold stronger against the followers of Jesus. They had prevailed nothing against Christ but must overthrow His followers, if possible. In every generation they must seek to ensnare those who would believe in Jesus. He related to his angels that Jesus had given His disciples power to rebuke them and cast them out, and to heal those whom they should afflict. Then Satan's angels went forth like roaring lions, seeking to destroy the followers of Jesus.

12

The Pentecost

When Jesus opened the understanding of the disciples to the meaning of the prophecies concerning himself, he assured them that all power was given him in Heaven and on earth, and bade them go preach the gospel to every creature. The disciples, with a sudden revival of their old hope that Jesus would take his place upon the throne of David at Jerusalem, inquired, "Wilt thou at this time restore again the kingdom to Israel?" The Saviour threw an uncertainty over their minds in regard to the subject by replying that it was not for them "to know the times or the seasons; which the Father hath put in his own power."

The disciples began to hope that the wonderful descent of the Holy Ghost would influence the Jewish people to accept Jesus. The Saviour forbore to farther explain, for he knew that when the Holy Spirit should come upon them in full measure their minds would be illuminated and they would fully understand the work before them, and take it up just where he had left it.

The disciples assembled in the upper chamber, uniting in supplications with the believing women, with Mary the mother of Jesus, and with his brethren. These brethren, who had been unbelieving, were now fully established in their faith by the scenes attending the crucifixion, and by the resurrection and ascension of the Lord. The number assembled was about one hundred and twenty.

"And when the day of Pentecost was fully come, they were all with one accord in one place. And suddenly there came a sound from heaven as of a rushing mighty wind, and it filled all the house where they were sitting. And there appeared unto them cloven tongues like as of fire, and it sat upon each of them. And they were all filled with the Holy Ghost, and began to speak with other tongues, as the Spirit gave them utterance." The Holy Ghost assuming the form of tongues of fire divided at the tips, and resting upon those assembled, was an emblem of the gift which was bestowed upon them of speaking with fluency several different languages, with which they had formerly been unacquainted. And the appearance of fire signified the fervent zeal with which they would labor, and the power which would attend their words.

Under this heavenly illumination, the scriptures which Christ had explained to them, stood forth in their minds with the vivid luster and loveliness of clear and powerful truth. The vail which had prevented them from seeing the end of that which was abolished was now removed, and the object of Christ's mission and the nature of his kingdom were comprehended with perfect clearness.

The Jews had been scattered to almost every nation, and spoke various languages. They had come long distances to Jerusalem, and had temporarily taken up their abode there, to remain through the religious festivals then in progress, and to observe their requirements. When assembled, they were of every known tongue. This diversity of languages was a great obstacle to the labors of God's servants in publishing the doctrine of Christ to the uttermost parts of the earth. That God should supply the deficiency of the apostles in a miraculous manner was to the people the most perfect confirmation of the testimony of these witnesses for Christ. The Holy Spirit had done for them that which they could not have accomplished for themselves in a lifetime; they could now spread the truth of the gospel abroad, speaking with accuracy the language of those for whom they were laboring. This miraculous gift was the highest evidence they could present to the world that their commission bore the signet of Heaven.

"And there were dwelling at Jerusalem Jews, devout men, out of every nation under heaven. Now when this was noised abroad, the multitude came together, and were confounded, because that every man heard them speak in his own language. And they were all amazed, and marveled, saying one to another, Behold, are not all these which speak Galileans? And how hear we every man in our own tongue, wherein we were born?"

The priests and rulers were greatly enraged at this wonderful manifestation, which was reported throughout all Jerusalem and the vicinity; but they dared not give way to their malice, for fear of exposing themselves to the hatred of the people. They had put the Master to death, but here were his servants, unlearned men of Galilee, tracing out the wonderful fulfillment of prophecy, and teaching the doctrine of Jesus in all the languages then spoken. They spoke with power of the wonderful works of the Saviour, and unfolded to their hearers the plan of salvation in the mercy and sacrifice of the Son of God. Their words convicted and converted thousands who listened. The traditions and superstitions inculcated by the priests were swept away from their minds, and they accepted the pure teachings of the Word of God.

Peter showed them that this manifestation was the direct fulfillment of the prophecy of Joel, wherein he foretold that such power would come upon men of God to fit them for a special work.

Peter traced back the lineage of Christ in a direct line to the honorable house of David. He did not use any of the teachings of Jesus to prove his true position, because he knew their prejudices were so great that it would be of no effect. But he referred them to David, whom the Jews regarded as a venerable patriarch of their nation. Said Peter:—

"For David speaketh concerning him, I foresaw the Lord always before my face; for he is on my right hand, that I should not be moved. Therefore did my heart rejoice, and my tongue was glad; moreover also my flesh shall rest in hope; because thou wilt not leave my soul in hell, neither wilt thou suffer thine Holy One to see corruption.

Peter here shows that David could not have spoken in reference to himself, but definitely of Jesus Christ. David died a natural death like other men; his sepulcher, with the honored dust it contained, had been preserved with great care until that time. David, as king of Israel, and also as a prophet, had been specially honored by God. In prophetic vision he was shown the future life and ministry of Christ. He saw his rejection, his trial, crucifixion, burial, resurrection, and ascension.

David testified that the soul of Christ was not to be left in hell (the grave), nor was his flesh to see corruption. Peter shows the fulfillment of this prophecy in Jesus of Nazareth. God had actually raised him up from the tomb before his body saw corruption. He was now the exalted One in the Heaven of heavens.

On that memorable occasion, large numbers who had heretofore ridiculed the idea of so unpretending a person as Jesus being the Son of God, became thoroughly convinced of the truth, and acknowledged him as their Saviour. Three thousand souls were added to the church. The apostles spoke by the power of the Holy Ghost; and their words could not be controverted, for they were confirmed by mighty miracles, wrought by them through the outpouring of the Spirit of God. The disciples were themselves astonished at the results of this visitation, and the quick and abundant harvest of souls. All the people were filled with amazement. Those who did not yield their prejudice and bigotry were so overawed that they dared not by voice or violence attempt to stay the mighty work, and, for the time being, their opposition ceased.

The arguments of the apostles alone, although clear and convincing, would not have removed the prejudice of the Jews which had withstood so much evidence. But the Holy Ghost sent those arguments home with divine power to their hearts. They were as sharp arrows of the Almighty, convicting them of their terrible guilt in rejecting and crucifying the Lord of glory. "Now when they heard this, they were pricked in their heart, and said unto Peter and to the rest of the apostles, Men and brethren, what shall we do? Then Peter said unto them, Repent, and be baptized every one of you in the name of Jesus Christ for the remission of sins, and ye shall receive the gift of the Holy Ghost."

Peter urged home upon the convicted people the fact that they had rejected Christ because they had been deceived by the priests and rulers; and if they continued to look to them for counsel, and waited for those leaders to acknowledge Christ before they dared to do so, they would never accept him. Those powerful men, although they made a profession of sanctity, were ambitious, and zealous for riches and earthly glory. They would never come to Christ to receive light. Jesus had foretold a terrible retribution to come upon that people for their obstinate unbelief, notwithstanding the most powerful evidences given them that Jesus was the Son of God.

From this time forth the language of the disciples was pure, simple, and accurate in word and accent, whether they spoke their native tongue or a foreign language. These humble men, who had never learned in the school of the prophets, presented truths so elevated and pure as to astonish those who heard them. They could not go personally to the uttermost parts of the earth; but there were men at the feast from every quarter of the world, and the truths received by them were carried to their various homes, and published among their people, winning souls to Christ.

This testimony in regard to the establishment of the Christian church is given us, not only as an important portion of sacred history, but also as a lesson. All who profess the name of Christ should be waiting, watching, and praying with one heart. All differences should be put away, and unity and tender love one for another pervade the whole. Then our prayers may go up together to our Heavenly Father with strong, earnest faith. Then we may wait with patience and hope the fulfillment of the promise.

The answer may come with sudden velocity and overpowering might; or it may be delayed for days and weeks, and our faith receive a trial. But God knows how and when to answer our prayer. It is *our* part of the work to put ourselves in connection with the divine channel. God is responsible for *his* part of the work. He is faithful who hath promised. The great and important matter with us is to be of one heart and mind, putting aside all envy and malice, and, as humble supplicants, to watch and wait. Jesus, our Representative and Head, is ready to do for us what he did for the praying, watching ones on the day of Pentecost.

Scriptural Index

What makes this set so popular?
The Results!
Lifechanging Results

The Bible Study Companion Set   *$59.95

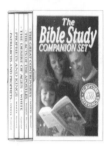

All five books together covering Genesis to Revelation — from the beginning of the universe through human history and on into our future. This set truly enriches your life with a better understanding of the Bible.

Patriarchs and Prophets

Where did the human race come from? Why do bad things happen to good people? Why are babies born sick, and why do so many hard-working people never seem to get ahead? If God is good, why doesn't He prevent sadness and heartbreak? And if He is all-powerful, why doesn't He do something about evil and sickness? These questions and many more are answered in this remarkable book. Patriarchs and Prophets has brought peace and hope to millions throughout the world. *US$11.99

Prophets and Kings

Beginning with King Solomon, this book recounts the stories of great men and women of the Bible who lived from his reign to the first advent of Jesus Christ. Here you will read of Elijah, Daniel, Isaiah, and Jeremiah, among others–and you will find the lessons God would have us all learn from their lives. *US$11.99

The Desire of Ages

This book is about the Man who stands at the center of all human history. No one else has had such a profound influence on the people of this planet as Jesus Christ. *US$11.99

The Acts of the Apostles

This book is about power–ultimate power. The awesome power of the Holy Spirit, and what He can do in human lives when we surrender to be used by Him. When Pentecost came upon the early church, what God's people accomplished was miraculous. And all that the apostles did, God wants to do again through us today. *US$11.99

The Great Controversy

The world is on the verge of a stupendous crisis. Here is the authoritative answer to the confusion and despair of this tense age. Revealing God's ultimate plan for mankind, The Great Controversy may be the most important book you'll ever read. *US$11.99

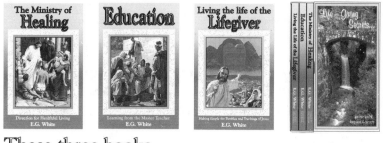

These three books
will change your life...
...Forever

The Life–Giving Secrets Set   *$29.95

This three volume set will help you in your understanding the whole being–Physical, mental, and spiritual. With over 2,200 spiritual references, this set will make it simple to understand these Life–giving secrets.

Living the Life of the Lifegiver

Here is the most compelling book ever written on the parables of Jesus. Through familiar objects and incidents—the harvest, the shepherd, the builder, the traveler, the homemaker—Jesus linked divine truth with the common and ordinary. As you read this book, you will experience the sensation of walking through a door into a previously unseen but very real world. *US$9.95

Education

This book clearly reveals that love, the basis of creation and redemption, is the basis of true education. Simply put, changes that last are those that are motivated by unselfish love. *US$9.95

The Ministry of Healing

Using Jesus Christ as the example of the true Medical Missionary, this book, first written over 80 years ago, is an extraordinary example of medical-science prophecy. Many topics, such as mind cures, natural remedies, vegetarian diet, exercise, prenatal influences, and health education, are covered. The author speaks of true health and healing in conjunction with the powers of the Great Physician, Jesus Christ. *US$9.95

*All prices include postage and handling

Credit card orders, call: 800-423-1319

Send check or money order to:
Remnant Publications
P.O. Box 426, Coldwater, MI 49036

ARE YOU SEARCHING FOR TRUTH?

Do you need reliable answers to urgent questions?

- *Can we know and understand the future?*
- *What are the tests of a true prophet?*
- *Is the development of character important?*
- *Are there physical and spiritual laws for health and happiness?*
- *What really happens to us after death?*
- *Is it possible to live forever?*
- *How can you find inner peace in a world of chaos?*

Discover the answers to these and other vital questions by enrolling in our Bible Correspondence Course. We care about you and your welfare. Thats why we prepared this series of thought-provoking Bible study lessons to help people just like you. These lessons will stimulate you to think independently, and help you conscientiously make the choices which will make you happy.

The first two lessons in the series are free of charge. If you like the lessons, we ask you to include a nominal freewill offering, beginning with lesson three, to help cover postage and handling.

Do You Want To Know More?

Yes, Please send me, at no charge, the first two lessons.

Name_____

Address_____

City_____ State_____ Zip_____

Send to:

Bible Correspondence Course
P.O. Box 426
Coldwater, MI 49036   AL99